OUR
LATIN
TABLE

OUR LATIN TABLE

CELEBRATIONS, RECIPES, AND MEMORIES

Fernando Saralegui

❋

INTRODUCTION BY Alvaro Saralegui

FOOD PHOTOGRAPHY BY Quentin Bacon

LIFESTYLE PHOTOGRAPHY BY Andrew French

Bulfinch Press

AOL Time Warner Book Group

Boston · New York · London

First Edition

Library of Congress Cataloging-in-Publication Data
Saralegui, Fernando.
    Our Latin table : celebrations, recipes, and memories /
Fernando Saralegui ; food photography by Quentin Bacon ;
lifestyle photography by Andrew French. —1st ed.
        p. cm.
    ISBN 0-8212-2854-4
    1. Cookery, Cuban. 2. Menus. I. Title.
TX716.C8S27 2003
641.597291—dc21   2003040427

Food Editor: Kathy Oberman

Design by Dania Davey

Bulfinch Press is a division of AOL Time Warner Book Group.

Printed in the United Kingdom

To Amy, Isabel, and Mateo,
my wonderful family,
for their love
and
to my larger family
and our table
that keeps us all together

———————————

In memory of Guido Alvarez: "Best of the best"

CONTENTS

ACKNOWLEDGMENTS

Our parents, Jorge and Titi Saralegui, 1952.

he journey that made food, wine, and hospitality my life began with a steady diet of Cuban and Spanish food at home, a variety of restaurant jobs with groundbreaking chefs, and good friends and mentors who fed me well. Although never a chef, I have spent most of my adult life in restaurants and now spend most of my free time at markets and wine stores, in the kitchen, and at our table. Over time so many people have been part of this journey and important to my life.

First, of course, our family—starting with the women who fed us: our mother, Titi, a talented and loving cook, and our grandmothers, Adelaida (Gui Gui) and Amalita, and our great-grandmother Carolina. And of course our father, Jorge, for getting us all here safely.

In the kitchen helping every day was our nanny, Francisca Quiroga (Tati). Along with feeding us she enthusiastically helped keep the seven of us in line.

My own generation—my brothers and sisters—all have recipes and love throughout these menus, including Maite and Jorge. Javier's friendship, energy, ideas, and coaching—both on the page and in the gym—along with Alvaro's support and experience made this book happen. Alejandro and Kendall gave their insightful ideas and suggestions. And our sister Luli, who has supported me in every way, has always graciously allowed her beautiful home to be the setting for our gatherings and once again opened her doors as the backdrop for this book.

Good friends like Andy French, our official family photographer, have made this book possible. Andy's art hung on the walls of my first restaurant; he photographed my wedding and our parents' forty-fifth wedding anniversary; and he beautifully captured our family for this book. His natural talent is outdone only by the grace he brings to everything he does.

Kathy Oberman, my food editor and longtime friend, brought the menus—with recipes from my restaurants, friends, and family—into focus. She made the deadlines possible, and I would go into a kitchen with her at my side anytime.

Fred Landman, whose support and friendship have made my restaurant and career possible, is always there for me rain or shine and the first to recognize a job well done. He is an epicure in the style of a time long past and is a dear friend.

Ted Max and Peter Svarre were both friends of my brother Javier first, and both have become trusted confidants and indispensable allies in business and at the Bar-B-Que.

Many of the dishes in this book came from collaborations with the chefs who passed through my second restaurant, L-Ray: Jimmy Bradley, Alex Garcia, Aaron Sanchez, John Decker, and Jorge Adriazola. Jorge was always available for questions and always brought with him his wonderful Peruvian aesthetic and good humor. And thanks to Douglas Rodriguez for lending me half these guys.

My experience with L-Ray brought me in touch with several people, all partners who helped me realize the vision of this pan-American neighborhood restaurant. Steven Abramowitz's English approach to my Latin passion was a perfect fit. Ed Koller's faith in me never falters and I count on it. Steven Bernstein is a brother entrepreneur extraordinaire. Bill Dye matched my energy and let everyone know "seventeen years, ladies and gentlemen, seventeen years." David Turner, my master carpenter, builds dreams for me and others and will always have a cold beer waiting for him.

Along the way I've been fortunate enough to come in contact with people who I feel are the best in the restaurant business. I cut my teeth at Chez Panisse, where I learned Alice Waters's natural approach to food and had a culinary awakening. Chez Panisse is my true alma mater. I met Mario Batali drinking grappa, and he's been a friend to me and my family ever since. If there is a more talented, happier, or more giving chef, I am not aware of him or her. I am lucky to have Mario in my corner.

Michael Skurnik and Nick Mautone are both great friends, Michael since "double chai" and Nick since we were busboys. Joe Bastianich has visited Austin and always has an infused something to try. Fred Eric in Los Angeles is insane and I would not want it any other way; we cross paths infrequently but always create memories. Bobby Flay was my restaurant neighbor and I take pride in having him as a colleague. Drew Nieporent is invaluable for all he does to promote our industry and New York City. Joshua Wesson of Best Cellars was kind enough to make all the wine suggestions for this book. Thank you.

My move to Austin brought me closer to my wife's family: Sandy, Skipper, and Macon. It also has created a new community of culinary friends. Valerie Goodwin has made my work at the Texas Hill Country Wine and Food Festival possible. Without her none of it gets done, including this book. Thanks also to John Pecore, Pam Blanton—a new friend for her support and talent—Mark Paul, Stewart Scruggs, Michael Vilim, Larry Peel, Miguel Ravago, Jim Johnson, Quincy Erickson, and our office intern Kathryn Biegel.

A special thanks to our team at Bulfinch Press. Our editor, Karen Murgolo, was indispensable in navigating this project into a reality and brought in Dania Davey, our book designer, and her elegant designs to the project. I am grateful to Jill Cohen for seeing the potential of the story we wanted to tell and to Betty Wong and Jared Silverman for getting the message. The Bulfinch team was also responsible for making Quentin Bacon part of the project. His eye makes the food look delicious with the help of his team: Darienne Sutton, Kevin Crafts, and his assistant Tina.

All of the above family and friends have helped make this book possible and are welcome at my table any day!

The current Saralegui family is composed of seven children whose grandfathers were both from the Basque country in Spain. At different times both men emigrated from Spain to Cuba. They exported big appetites for excitement while maintaining strong ties to their Iberian heritage.

Our grandfather Abuelo Saralegui was the president of the Centro Vasco, a Basque society in Cuba, best known perhaps for its restaurant. He never cooked much of anything, but he did love what others cooked for him. Our other grandfather, Manolo Goicolea, was born in Guernica, Spain, a city made infamous by Hitler and famous by Picasso. Manolo moved to Cuba when he was twenty but still enjoyed his favorite Basque dish, porruzalda (a leeks, potatoes, and salt cod soup), decades later.

Our grandfathers became fond of Latin food almost instantly. The tendency for immigrants to develop a love for different foods in their new country while maintaining a taste for the cuisine from their country of origin has been replayed in the United States many times. Interestingly, the new food often finds it way onto the dinner table of the host country. Potstickers, sushi, pasta, and tacos are a testament to this phenomenon in the United States. The new immigrants become acculturated to their adopted country while simultaneously having a cultural impact on it.

Our family escaped from Cuba in 1960 while Fidel Castro consolidated his power on the island. We settled in Bronxville, New York, a suburb of New York City. Feeding seven children and various relatives, daily, required a methodical approach and an appreciation for shortcuts. Hence, "American" food became a larger part of many of our meals. We ate an unusual diet:

a combination of traditional Cuban and 1960s American packaged foods. The guava paste shared shelf space with Velveeta cheese. Fusion was born.

That is not to say we kids took to fusion right away. Canned sweet ham sometimes went uneaten. Ropa vieja, a shredded beef dish, often stayed on a plate for hours waiting to be eaten. Flan de coco and Oreos were favorites, while eating purée de papa (a type of mashed potatoes) and spinach was delayed as long as possible. We were fickle eaters, but we were evenhanded in our fickleness.

We were fortunate that both of our parents went to college in the United States and hence were familiar with many American customs. However, they did not know anything about American middle-school hazing rituals. We sometimes had to hide our Latin lunches to save ourselves from ridicule. We lived quite close to school and most often walked home for lunch. Soup was always served as a first course, as was the case in Cuba. The main course, however, was often American cheeseburgers cooked by our nanny, Tati. Many friends would tag along to our house for lunch to eat the famous Pan-Cheese Burgers.

About twenty years later our home became even more popular as our friends started drinking cocktails. They knew Cuba as a little country whose GNP was small and whose exports were forbidden. However, Cuban cocktail recipes had made their way to American shores decades before the embargo. First there was one of Hemingway's favorites,

the daiquiri. Next is the drink that may replace the margarita, the mojito, a cocktail with mint leaves that should be consumed at the Kentucky Derby but is not—yet. Lastly, the fusion drink that screams out *America* and *Cuba* is the rum and Coke, a drink consumed around the world.

We ourselves began to explore new foods outside of American and Cuban food as we left home for college and jobs in the real world. Mexican food's popularity was booming, and though much spicier than Cuban food, we consumed copious amounts. My wife and I visited my older brother, Jorge, in San Francisco and ate Ecuadorian ceviche for the first time. We paid a visit to our parents in Miami, had lunch with their Colombian friends, and ate arepas. Latin American food was becoming American food.

As the seven of us spread out over the United States (our youngest sister, Luli, went as far as Munich), we made a more conscious decision to meet regularly. To date, three of us have homes in Bridgehampton, New York, and three of us live on the West Coast, but we get together for holidays, birthdays, and other celebrations. These times together bring the comforting sounds, aromas, and flavors of our childhood, reminding us we are still a Cuban family.

The next generation of Saraleguis adds even more flavor to the cultural melting pot that is America. Their Spanish is mediocre at best, though we all are determined to improve their ability. The kids love guacamole, fried plantains or tostones, and black bean soup.

They are proud when Cuba is in the news, yet they know more about troubles in the Middle East.

The experiences described on the following pages talk to the influence America has had on our family and the influence we have had on our community. This interaction is happening all across the country. Americans already consume more salsa than ketchup. Over the next ten years we are willing to bet much of what is in this book will be viewed less as a peek into celebrations of a lucky family from Cuba and more as a description of the new mainstream lifestyle.

Working with Fernando on this book has enriched our family. We feel strongly that the melding of Latin American and United States cultures through music, décor, language, fashion, and food will enrich us yet again.

Fernando is one of my younger brothers, and the author of this book. He has done a wonderful job of pulling together the best recipes from our family and from his professional career.

After a distinguished career in bartending at a young age, Fernando's ambition eventually took him past the world of margaritas and cosmopolitans and to Manhattan. In New York he launched two restaurants, Alva and L-Ray, where he stirred together all of his experiences and talent in cooking, architecture, design, and mixology to great success. Opportunity and two new kids led him to Austin, Texas, his wife, Amy's, home state. There he was Director of the Texas Hill Country Wine and Food Festival and still a source of humor and good food at his table.

Salud!

—ALVARO SARALEGUI

A Latin Pantry

I think most people will be surprised about how comfortable they already are with the ingredients of a Latin pantry. Sure, there are those funny-sounding root vegetables and bananas, but once you get past the names we basically use them like potatoes. A translation of a handful of terms, dishes, and ingredients will help, but once again, most cooks are familiar with poblanos and chorizo. Truth be known, if you've got some garlic, lime, black beans, and rice you're well on your way!

ESSENTIAL INGREDIENTS TO HAVE ON HAND IF YOU WANT TO COOK WITH LATIN FLAVOR

- Arborio rice
- Avocados
- Black beans
- Canned green chilies
- Chorizo
- Cornhusks
- Cornmeal
- Cumin
- Flat-leaf parsley
- Frozen yucca (cassava)
- Garlic
- Green bell peppers
- Guava jelly
- Guava paste
- Jalapeños
- Lemons
- Limes
- Manchego cheese
- Mangoes
- Mint
- Monterey Jack cheese
- Olive oil
- Olives with pimiento
- Oranges
- Oregano
- Plantains
- Queso blanco
- Red bell pepper
- Red wine vinegar
- Roasted red peppers
- Spanish olives
- Spanish onion
- White rice

Avocado.

APREPAS Corn cakes made with cornmeal.

AVOCADOS A rich green fruit with pebbly green-black skin. To peel, pit, and dice an avocado, take an avocado and slice vertically into it, rolling knife around the fruit using the pit as a pivot. Grasp the fruit with both hands on each side of the slice and rotate each side in opposite directions, separating the halves. One side will retain the nut. Holding that half in your palm, carefully strike the nut with the blade of your knife; with the blade lodged in the nut, twist and remove nut. With half the fruit still in your palm, use the knife tip to score the flesh horizontally and vertically. Using a tablespoon, carefully work between the skin and flesh, using the skin as a guide; follow the curve of the fruit. As the flesh separates from the skin, gently let the scored cubes come apart into a medium bowl. Haas avocados are small and deep green in color. They possess a more refined taste and texture.

BACALAO Salted cod.

BELL PEPPERS, ROASTED The traditional way to roast this mild, sweet pepper is directly over the open flame of a gas stove, turning until completely charred on all sides. If you do not have a gas stove, slice the peppers in half, core and seed them, and lay them on a baking sheet. Place the baking sheet under the broiler and broil until charred. The nice thing about doing them this way is that you can roast several peppers at one time. Cool in brown paper bag and peel by rubbing your thumbs over the flesh.

BONIATO Cuban sweet potato with red mottled skin and white flesh and a nutty sweet flavor.

CALDO GALLEGO Traditional white bean soup from the Galician province of Spain.

CEVICHE Raw seafood cocktail "cooked" in citrus acid.

CHIMICHURRI Argentinean spicy garlic herb oil used on cooked meats.

CHIPOTLE PEPPER A dried jalapeño, brick in color, with smoky flavor. They are also sold hydrated in cans.

CHORIZO Spicy Spanish sausage seasoned with paprika and garlic, available cured or fresh.

EMPANADA A pastry folded over with a myriad of fillings, served throughout Latin America.

FLAN A baked custard covered with a burnt-sugar syrup.

GUAVA Oval to pear-shaped fruit found throughout the tropics, used to make sweet and tangy paste and jelly.

JALAPEÑOS Cooks should use rubber gloves while preparing fresh jalapenos. The heat from the pepper will burn eyes and nostrils and lips if touched by hands after cutting and dicing without gloves. Including the seeds makes the recipe hotter.

JICAMA Tuber in varied shapes and sizes with a waxy brown skin, an apple-texture flesh, and a celery-and-pear flavor.

MALANGA A yellow-brown tuber with rough skin with concentric seams and a nutty flavor boiled and fried. Similar to taro root.

MANCHEGO A semi-hard Parmesan-type cheese with a pale brown wax casing.

MANGO A rich, tropical fruit, which has an oddly shaped pit that clings to the flesh. To pit a mango, use a sharp knife to cut the mango lengthwise just off the center and then slice off the remaining side. With one half of the mango in the palm of your hand, slice the flesh lengthwise into 4 or 5 slices. Use the knife to slip under the flesh and remove it from the skin.

MARIQUITAS Fried semi-ripe plantain chips sliced thin.

MASA HARINA A coarse cornmeal.

MIGAS A Tex-Mex scrambled-egg dish.

MOJO A sauce made from freshly squeezed orange and lime juices, olive oil, garlic, fresh oregano, and cumin. Mojo can be used as a condiment for fish, chicken, and meat. Use mortar and pestle to grind garlic with oregano and cumin. Transfer the mixture to a nonreactive bowl and stir in the orange and lime juices. Using a whisk, slowly mix the olive oil into the sauce to emulsify.

NATILLA Sweet vanilla custard.

PANCETTA Italian fresh bacon.

PICADILLO A Cuban spiced ground-beef dish.

PINEAPPLE A sweet fruit common in Latin desserts. To remove the core, cut the pineapple in half horizontally, giving you two whole rounds. Cut the pineapple halves in half lengthwise and again into quarters. Cut off the center core. Continue to cut these pieces in half again lengthwise. You should now have 16 spears of pineapple. Pineapple can be cut a few hours in advance and kept in the refrigerator in an airtight nonreactive container.

PLANTAINS A banana with varied preparations depending on ripeness of fruit: green to yellow for tostones and mariquitas, black for fried sweet plantains. This type of banana is treated like a vegetable rather than a fruit because of its toughness. When plantain is green (not ripe), cut off the ends and make a lengthwise slit on the skin. While holding the plantain steady with one hand, use the other hand to slide the tip of the knife under the skin and begin to pull it away, going from top to bottom. Soak peeled plantains in salted water. Drain on a paper towel.

POBLANO PEPPER A dark green pepper with medium heat often stuffed for chile rellenos.

QUESO FRESCO BLANCO A fresh unripened farmer cheese used throughout Latin America.

ROPA VIEJA Literally "old clothes," a shredded beef dish.

SOFRITO The holy trinity of Latin cookery: garlic, onion, and green bell peppers.

SPANISH ONION A yellow onion.

TAMALE A cornmeal dish similar to polenta often stuffed with meat or vegetables and wrapped like a small gift in a cornhusk or banana leaf. America's large Mexican population has made cornhusks easy to find, but in Cuba you're as likely to find boiled tamales wrapped like a square gift in a banana leaf.

TOMATILLO A Mexican green tomato, the tomatillo is encased in a paper-thin husk that resembles a Japanese lantern. To use, remove sticky husk and rinse in warm water. The flavor is fruity and acidic.

YUCA A waxy brown-skinned tuber with white flesh, prepared peeled and boiled.

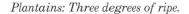

Plantains: Three degrees of ripe.

A Cuban Bar

All humans are social animals—Cubans maybe more so than others! We like to get together with friends and family to talk, eat, drink, and dance the night away. Growing up, we all have one shared memory: our parents having parties that began with seemingly endless cocktail hours. As children, we were kept awake by the revelry and would check in on the activities by sneaking peeks from the stairs.

This love of a party made pre-Castro Havana a destination for Americans. These social pilgrimages to Cuba resulted in the importing of exotic cocktails fueled with rum and tropical fruits to the United States. The result is that the American bar owes much to concoctions from south of the border.

My brothers and sisters all inherited this social tradition; however, it has to be said that I took it to heart. When I was fourteen, I asked my father to teach me the basics of the bar and he proudly took me under his wing. With the fundamentals in hand, I began what became an almost twenty-year career in bartending that led to my two restaurants. When the restaurant opportunities arrived, my convivial family jumped in and we all became partners in a new chapter of entertaining friends and family.

To put together your own bar you'll need a few things. Keep in mind that most of these items will last and are only used a bit at a time or have other uses in the kitchen. This includes the liquor. Unless you have large gatherings like we do, you'll be surprised how far a good bottle of tequila or rum will go, not to mention triple sec or Cointreau. One thing that will always come in handy are limes. Whenever you go the store, a dozen limes should be on your list.

EQUIPMENT

CLASSIC COCKTAIL SHAKER: Mine is a prized possession. With a few exceptions, I always prefer a shaken drink over a blended one. Always shake vigorously to both chill and meld ingredients, and yes—the over-your-shoulder shake works best! Depending on your shaker, you may also need a strainer to strain out ice while you pour your drink. Note: Always strain your cocktail over fresh ice. The ice you made the drink with is in the process of melting because of the shaking friction. Serving over fresh ice will prevent a watery or diluted drink.

2-OUNCE JIGGER: for measuring portions until you learn to eye the right amount

BLENDER: for frozen drinks

PARING KNIFE: for cutting fruit

CUTTING BOARD: for cutting fruit

MUDDLE: to mash fruit; alternatively, you can use a spoon

GLASSWARE: I'm not a stickler about glassware. A wineglass or wide highball glass will work for most cocktails, unless you take your cocktails "up," in which case you'll need a martini glass. You'll also need a pitcher for sangrias; however, (in a pinch) a bowl will do.

LIQUOR

TEQUILA AND RUM: These two spirits are the foundations of tropical cocktails. Tequila is made from the *piña,* or heart, of the blue agave and only from the appellation of Tequila in Mexico. Rum is made from sugarcane and is produced everywhere from Venezuela to Bermuda. Tequila and rum can both be aged to soften and meld flavors, creating a more mellow and rich product perfect for sipping straight. Unless otherwise noted, I prefer unaged or moderately aged spirits to create cocktails. When an *añejo,* or aged spirit, is used in a cocktail, its creamy nature is redundant and lost in the sugars. The aging process adds value to the product, so don't waste your money, unless you're sipping and savoring.

Age Designations

White or silver label: not aged
Gold label: colored with caramel to soften the flavor; makes a good margarita
Reposado: A "rested" spirit that has been in oak barrels from two months to one year. Clearly labeled as such.
Añejo: Aged for at *least* one year in sealed oak barrels. Clearly labeled as such.

CACHACA: A native from Brazil made from fermented and distilled sugarcane.

VODKA: Martinis are always cool and easily given a Latin twist (or jalapeño).

BLENDED SCOTCH: Not such a surprise. I have never met a Cuban gentleman who doesn't like to sip "we-key" over a few rocks.

ORANGE-BASED LIQUEURS: Triple sec, Cointreau, and Grand Marnier. Interchangeable; a matter of taste and price.

FRUIT LIQUEURS: Crème de banane and strawberry liqueur to intensify the fruit flavor in daiquiris.

JUICES

LIME, ORANGE, AND TOMATO

CANNED TROPICAL JUICES: Use for flavored margaritas and daiquiris: apricot, guava, pineapple, papaya, and mango.

CANNED COCONUT WATER

MIXERS

SODAS: Coca-Cola and club soda

SIMPLE SYRUP: A simple fifty-fifty mixture of water and granulated cane sugar. Stir together over light flame until all sugar is dissolved; let cool. Can be refrigerated for future use.

TABASCO SAUCE: There are other hot sauces; but this is the one for a classic cocktail.

WORCESTERSHIRE SAUCE: Can't make a bloody without it.

GRENADINE: The "rise" in sunrise.

COCO LÓPEZ: A must for piña coladas.

FROZEN LIMEADE: Should always be in the freezer because you never know when the mood will strike you.

GARNISHES

FRUIT: All kinds—orange, apple, grapes, pineapple, and melon for sangrias

LIMES: Always fresh and unblemished. Use blemished soft fruit for juice.

MINT: Fresh and unblemished

SPANISH STUFFED OLIVES, JALAPEÑOS

KOSHER SALT: Salt is one of the most misunderstood elements of a margarita. Regular iodized salt is wrong. Pebbly sea salt does not dissolve well, and you end up with a crunchy drink. When salting the glass, moisten the rim with a lime that has been squeezed. Dip the glass into salt that has been spread over a plate and jiggle to cover the rim well. Pick up the glass upside down at a forty-five-degree angle with one hand and, using the forefinger of your other hand, circle the inside of the rim, letting the excess salt fall out. This procedure stops a well-filled margarita from coming into contact with the salt, creating a salty drink. I always clear a section of the salted rim so I can catch the salt on the edge of my mouth to punctuate the cocktail. You may have detected that we take our cocktails seriously in this family!

"Latin" Rhythms

These music choices are not definitive and are certainly not all Latin, but to us they have the right vibe to cook, eat, party, and bring family and friends together.

Ali Farka Toure, with Ry Cooder, *Talking Timbuktu*

Arturo Sandoval, anything from him

Bailar Con Cuba, 6. "Pare Cochero— Órchestra Aragón"

Bossa Cuca Nova, *Revisited Classics*

Buena Vista Social Club with Ry Cooder, *Buena Vista Social Club*

Cal Tjader, *Verve Jazz Masters 39* or anything from him

Celia Cruz, *Cocktail Hour*

"Chano" Pozo, anything from him

Charlie Byrd, *Bossa Nova Pelos Passaros*

Cigar Music, *Tobacco Songs from Old Havana*

Claude Challe, *Buddha Bar II*

David Byrne, *Brazil Classics, Volumes 1, 2, 3*

David Byrne, *Rei Momo*

Esquival, Ultra Lounge series, *Space Age Bachelor Pad*

Gato Barbieri, *Gato Barbieri's Finest Hour*

Gloria Estefan, *Abriendo Puertas*

Havana Now! *The Havana Sessions*

Herb Alpert, *Definitive Hits*

Herbie Mann, *Flautista!*

Jesús Alemañy, *¡Cubanisimo!*

João Bosco, *As Mil E Uma Aldeias*

Los Lobos, *Kiko*

Los Super Seven, *Canto*, 8. "Teresa"

Mambo Kings (soundtrack)

Manu Chao, *Proxima Estación*, "Esperanza"

Mario Bauzá, anything from him

Mercedes Sosa, *30 Años*

Mongo Santamaria, *Olé Ola*

Nina Simone, anything from her

Ozomatli, *Embrace the Chaos*, 1. "Pa Lante"

Pancho Sanchez, *Freedom Sound*

Pedro Luis Ferrer, *Havana Caliente*

Perez Prado, *Havana, 3:00 am*

Putumayo Presents, *Cape Verde*

Rubén Blades and Willie Colon, *Tras La Tormenta*

Ry Cooder, Manuel Galbán, *Mambo Sinuendo*

Santana, *Black Magic Woman*

Sergio Mendes, *Brasileiro*

Tito Puente, anything from him

Ultra Lounge Vol. 2: *Mambo Fever*

Vince Guaraldi, *In Person*

Vince Guaraldi, *A Charlie Brown Christmas* (I just like this one)

Yma Sumac, anything from her

The Menus

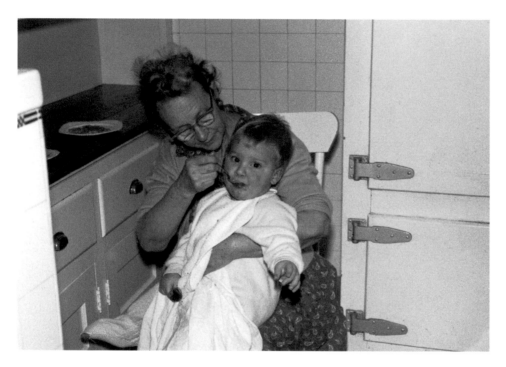

The author with his great-grandmother Carolina and a good appetite.

CELEBRATIONS, RECIPES, MEMORIES

Our table has always been the center of our home and our family. When we arrived in New York from Cuba we were five children soon to be seven, and it was the dinner table, holiday meals, and family celebrations that kept us together. We were nourished with stories, family, friends, and tradition.

Whether someone was in from out of town or it was a special birthday, people began to gather at our house. These events were often all-day affairs starting just after noon and ending long after we children had gone to sleep. As the day unfolded with a rising harmony of voices, music, and laughter, the fragrance of roasting meats, garlic, and citrus soon infused the house. The older kids helped our mother pull out the extra leaves of our dining table, while the younger kids were tossed about and smothered with love.

All seven of us inherited this sociability, took it with us, and shared it with others as we started to make our way in the world. Although most of the family followed our father into media, surely a convivial calling, I took being social a bit more seriously and started working in restaurants. Wherever I worked, the family brought their friends and expense accounts. Soon, together we owned restaurants, and as we began to settle down we all doubled our efforts to get together whenever possible.

I think the first dining table bought by our generation was by our older sister Maite. She was also the first to have children, and this new generation brought us all to their home often. She and her husband, Starrett, both went to school in Spain and are great cooks—

their table has been put to good use. As we all tied the knot we were drawn together to share the recipes from our lives at our growing table.

The influences on our table are many. Being Cuban there are Spanish, Basque, and, of course, Cuban dishes, but we've also included Mexican, Peruvian, and American recipes in our celebrations. Our travel and experiences have been incorporated throughout our menus as we simplified and created variations. The result is a repertoire of plates that are friendly and approachable.

We hope this collection of recipes and drinks along with memories of meals shared at our table will bring your family and friends together at yours and bring a bit of mambo into your kitchen.

Our family visiting our cousins in Florida, 1965.

New Year's Eve

My brother Javier's godfather, Guido Alvarez, who loved to entertain and be entertained, used to give a great New Year's Eve party for the family and one hundred or so other "close friends." Our family tries to celebrate New Year's Eve together in Guido's memory. Though not all of us make it to this party, we still call each other, without fail, on this night.

Traditionally, we drink Cuba Libres (page 75) while we cook this meal because New Year's was the day Castro took power. And if you're Cuban, you believe a free Cuba is in your future.

MENU

FRIED SWEET PLANTAINS

HEARTS OF PALM SALAD
WITH CHAMPAGNE VINAIGRETTE

CALDO GALLEGO

PORK TAMALES

MASHED YUCA

GUAVA BAKED HAM

COCONUT FLAN

SPARKLING SANGRIA

HAVANAPOLITANS

Opposite: Pork Tamales.

SERVES 12

Fried Sweet Plantains

3   cups olive oil

5   ripe (black) plantains, peeled and sliced into thick lengths like
    thick French fries

Heat the olive oil in a medium saucepan over medium-high heat until
hot but not smoking. In batches, fry the sliced plantain until crisp
and golden brown. Using a slotted spoon, remove the plantain to a
paper-towel-covered plate to drain. Keep the plate in a warm oven
until ready to serve.

Hearts of Palm Salad with Champagne Vinaigrette

VINAIGRETTE

1   cup olive oil

$^3/_4$ cup champagne vinegar

6   tablespoons fresh lemon juice

5   cloves garlic, minced

Salt and pepper to taste

SALAD

2   14-ounce cans hearts of palm, drained, cut into rounds

2   13.75-ounce cans artichokes, drained, quartered

1   cucumber, peeled, seeded, and sliced

1   small red onion, finely diced

2   heads curly endive or chicory, washed and dried

New Year's Eve. Kendall; Alvaro's wife, Lisa;
Fernando's wife, Amy (seated); and Fernando.

In a small container with lid, place the olive oil, vinegar, lemon juice,
garlic, salt, and pepper. Seal the lid tightly and shake vigorously until
well combined. Taste and adjust seasoning. Set aside. Vinaigrette can
be made up to 1 week ahead and kept in the refrigerator.

    In a nonreactive bowl, combine the hearts of palm, artichoke,
cucumber, and red onion. Toss with the vinaigrette to coat evenly.
Arrange a few leaves of the curly endive or chicory on individual
salad plates and top with vegetables. Serve immediately.

Party in the house. Mateo and Isabel.

Caldo Gallego—a garlic bean
soup—is from the Galician
side of our family (both our
grandmothers). This soup
was a winter staple in our
house and warms the soul.

Caldo Gallego

10 ounces dried white or navy beans

½ cup olive oil

¾ pound chorizo, sliced into ¼-inch pieces

7 cloves garlic, minced

2 carrots, finely chopped

2 stalks celery, finely chopped

1 large Spanish onion, finely diced

12 cups chicken stock

2 bay leaves

1 teaspoon dried thyme

1 ham hock or bone

2 heads kale, washed and chopped, hard stems removed

2 cups potatoes, diced

Salt and pepper to taste

Carefully pick through the beans and remove any foreign objects.
Soak overnight covered with water. Place beans in a colander and
rinse under cold water.

In a large, heavy stockpot, heat half of the olive oil over medium-
high heat, add chorizo, cook 3 minutes, remove, and reserve. Heat
the remaining olive oil and add garlic, carrot, celery, and onion to
the stockpot. Cook until soft, then add chicken stock, bay leaves,
thyme, ham hock, and beans, bring to a boil, and reduce heat to low.
Allow soup to simmer for 2 hours or until reduced by one quarter.
Remove ham hock or bone and bay leaves.

To the soup in the stockpot add the kale, potatoes, chorizo, salt,
and pepper and cook over medium heat for an additional half hour.
Taste and adjust seasoning.

The soup can be made up to 3 days in advance and kept
refrigerated in an airtight container.

Though this dish is found throughout Latin America, it's only since Amy and Starrett, both Texans, married into the family that the Mexican tradition of tamales on New Year's Eve has been embraced by our family, along with black-eyed peas.

Lisa, Amy, Fernando, Alvaro, Alejandro, and Angela.

Pork Tamales

FILLING

3   tablespoons olive oil

3   cloves garlic, minced

1   medium onion, chopped

1   pound ground pork, cooked

1   cup corn

¾   cup raisins

1   roasted pepper, diced

1   roasted green pepper, diced

2   tablespoons brown sugar

2   tablespoons cider vinegar

1   teaspoon cumin

Salt and pepper to taste

DOUGH

4   cups masa harina

2   teaspoons baking powder

2   teaspoons salt

14   tablespoons shortening or lard, chilled and cut into small pieces

2¼ cups warm chicken stock

48 dry cornhusks, soaked in water for 2 hours

Kitchen string

Prepare filling: Heat oil in heavy skillet and cook garlic and onion until soft, about 3 minutes. Add the rest of the filling ingredients and cook for 3 minutes. Cover with plastic wrap and set aside.

To make the dough, combine the masa, baking powder, and salt in a large mixing bowl. Add the shortening or lard to the dry mix and toss to coat the pieces. Using your fingers, rub the shortening or lard into the dry mix until it forms a rough cornmeal texture. Add the warm chicken stock, mixing to form dough. It may be necessary to add water 1 tablespoon at a time, until the dough holds together but is not sticky. Divide the dough evenly into 24 pieces.

On a clean, dry kitchen towel, place two cornhusks (vertically with wide sides touching) next to each other, overlapping an inch.

Arrange the tamale dough on the center seam of the husks. Place your filling in the center of the dough. Fold the bottom of the tamale a quarter of the way up toward the top, and then fold one side into the center to cover the filling and fold second side overlapping the first side. Tie the tamale closed with kitchen string.

In a saucepan, bring water to a boil over medium-high heat. Place the tamales in a steamer basket, cover, and steam for 40–45 minutes.

NOTE: America's large Mexican population has made cornhusks easy to find, but in Cuba you're as likely to find boiled tamales wrapped like a square gift in a banana leaf.

MAKES 24 TAMALES

Mashed Yuca

3   pounds frozen yuca

3   cloves garlic, minced

2   teaspoons dried oregano

½   cup (1 stick) unsalted butter

Salt and pepper to taste

Steam the yuca until just soft, about 30 minutes. In a large bowl, mash the yuca with garlic, oregano, butter, salt, and pepper. Serve immediately.

Guava Baked Ham

8-to-10-pound ham with bone

2   cups guava jelly

1   cup Coca-Cola

Preheat oven to 350 degrees.

Rinse ham under cold water and pat dry with paper towel. In a small bowl, whisk jelly and Coke together until well combined.

Kendall.

Traditions of the American South join a Cuban's favorite fruit to make the perfect ham glaze.

Score the skin of the ham in a diamond pattern with a sharp knife. Place the ham in a roasting pan and brush the guava glaze over it, coating it completely. Bake for 20 minutes until glaze is baked in. Then cover ham with aluminum foil and bake for another 40 minutes, basting with remaining glaze every 10 minutes.

Remove ham from roasting pan and allow to rest for 5 minutes. Slice the ham from the bone and serve immediately.

Coconut Flan

1¾ cup sugar

¾ cup shredded sweetened coconut

1½ cup whole milk

½ cup unsweetened coconut milk

¼ teaspoon salt

3 eggs

3 egg yolks

1 tablespoon vanilla

Preheat oven to 350 degrees.

In a heavy saucepan, melt 1 cup sugar over medium-high heat, stirring occasionally, until it is amber in color and a smooth liquid. Immediately remove from heat and pour into the bottom of heated 9-inch glass pie plate, a 2-quart casserole, or a heavy cake mold. (To heat the pie plate, pour hot or boiling water into it and let it stand for a minute or two, then drain and dry completely before adding the sugar syrup.) Tilt the dish to cover the bottom of the pan completely with the sugar syrup. Sprinkle the shredded coconut evenly over the sugar syrup. Set aside.

In a heavy saucepan, bring the milk, coconut milk, and salt to a boil over medium heat and remove from heat immediately.

In a large mixing bowl, beat together the eggs, egg yolks, remaining sugar, and vanilla until pale yellow in color. While the beater is running on high, slowly add ½ cup of the hot milk mixture and beat until eggs are tempered. Slowly add the remaining hot milk and continue beating for 30 seconds.

We think that Coconut Flan was our mother's tastiest dessert. It's a favorite at all our special occasions.

Pour the mixture over the syrup and coconut and place the dish in a shallow roasting pan. Fill the pan three quarters full with warm water, or halfway up the flan dish. Place in oven and cook for 1 hour.

Remove from oven and carefully remove flan dish from hot water. While the flan is still warm, run a knife around the edge to loosen it from the sides of the dish if necessary.

To remove flan, place a plate on top of the dish and invert the flan onto the plate. Make sure the plate is large enough to hold the flan and has enough of a well to hold the syrup.

Flan can be served warm or chilled. It can be prepared 2 days in advance and kept covered and refrigerated.

Sparkling Sangria

1   bottle (375 ml) white rum
1   pint apple juice
1   pint grapefruit juice
1   pint pineapple juice
2   green apples, cored and sliced
1/2   pineapple, cored, sliced,
      and sectioned
1   bunch seedless green grapes, halved
4   bottles sparkling wine—
      try an Italian spumante

Combine all ingredients in a pitcher, except the sparkling wine. Just before your guests arrive, add the sparkling wine (this will assist in retaining the sangria's sparkle). Chill. Serve in a wineglass garnished with a slice of apple.

Havanapolitan

2   ounces white rum
1   ounce Cointreau
1   ounce lime juice
1   ounce cranberry juice
Fresh mint sprigs
Ice

Combine rum, Cointreau, lime juice, and cranberry juice with ice in a shaker and shake. Strain into a chilled martini glass and garnish with a sprig of mint.

Good Luck Fishing Trip

Javier and I loved to fish for snapper and grouper as kids in Key Biscayne, Florida, but our collective time in the wild as adults can be summed up with our L.L. Bean catalog reading. When the weather is stormy we grab the fishing rods, and if we get lucky, it's a reason to party.

Javier and Fernando making the most of a stormy day.

MENU

**STEAMED WHOLE SNAPPER L-RAY
WITH MUSSELS AND CORN
WITH A LIME-CHILI-COCONUT BROTH
IN BANANA LEAF**

MANGO AND MINT SALAD

SARALEGUI BLACK BEAN GUACAMOLE

**CHILLED CLAMS ON
THE HALF SHELL WITH SANGRITA**

ALVARO'S FROZEN LIME DAIQUIRIS

WINE
SPANISH RUEDA
(BODEGAS ANGEL LORENZO CACHAZO)

SPANISH CAMPO DE BORJA
(BODEGAS BORSAO)

SERVES 6

Make every effort in creating the banana leaf envelope for this snapper dish, because when it's opened, the first waft of fragrance will be like nothing you've ever smelled before.

Steamed Whole Snapper L-Ray with Mussels and Corn with a Lime-Chili-Coconut Broth in Banana Leaf

2   tablespoons vegetable oil

1   medium white onion, thinly sliced

3   jalapeños, ribs and seeds removed, diced

1   cup white wine

$\frac{1}{2}$ cup of fresh lime juice

2   cups unsweetened coconut milk

6   banana leaves

1   3-pound whole snapper, scaled, gutted, and gills removed

3–4 fresh ears of corn, husked and kernels removed,
       or 3–4 cups frozen corn

1   small zucchini, julienned

1   small summer squash, julienned

1   medium carrot, peeled and julienned

Salt and pepper to taste

1   quart of fresh mussels, scrubbed cleaned and beards removed

$1\frac{1}{4}$ cup chopped cilantro

1   lime, cut into wedges

Preheat oven to 450 degrees.

In a medium saucepan, heat vegetable oil until hot but not smoking. Add onion and jalapeños and cook for 3–4 minutes. Add the white wine, lime juice, and coconut milk and cook for an additional 3 minutes. Remove the broth from heat and pour into a large roasting pan.

Spread the banana leaves evenly in the center of the roasting pan and place the whole snapper in the center. Sprinkle the corn kernels, zucchini, squash, and carrot over the fish and season with salt and pepper.

At my restaurant L-Ray, I was lucky to have a chef who was talented and a friend. Jorge Adriazola, a good Basque name, had a lot to be proud of, including this snapper dish.

Bring the ends of each leaf together over the fish, creating a tent effect; use a toothpick or wooden skewer to hold leaves in place. Cover the pan with aluminum foil and bake for 15 minutes per inch of the snapper's thickness, measured at the thickest part of the fish.

During the final 5 minutes of cooking, add mussels directly into the broth at bottom of roasting pan, cover again, and return to oven for remaining cooking time.

Remove the pan from the oven and lift the fish from the roasting pan, holding the top of the leaf envelope. Place the fish package on a deep serving platter and pour the mussels and broth around it. Remove skewers to unwrap fish just before serving.

To serve the fish, gently cut along the length of the backbone. Divide it into 3 equal portions between the head and tail. Using a fork, gently separate each portion from the bone. Using your hands, lift the bone out of the remaining fish fillet and cut 3 more portions.

Spoon broth over each portion of fish and add 3 or 4 mussels. Garnish with fresh cilantro and a wedge of lime.

NOTE: Grouper or other medium-size white fish will also work.

Mango and Mint Salad

Although it may sound exotic, this salad could not be simpler or more refreshing.

3   ripe mangoes, sliced

2   limes, juiced

1   clove garlic, minced

$\frac{1}{4}$ cup honey

$\frac{1}{4}$ cup mint leaves, shredded

To pit the mango, use a sharp knife to cut the mango lengthwise just off the center and then slice off the remaining side. With one half of the mango in the palm of your hand, slice the flesh lengthwise into 4–5 slices. Use the knife to slip under the flesh and remove it from the skin.

To serve individually, plate ½ mango per guest. Whisk lime juice, garlic, and honey in a nonreactive bowl; drizzle over fruit, and sprinkle with mint.

Saralegui Black Bean Guacamole

1   cup frozen corn, roasted

1   cup canned black beans, rinsed

½   cup diced Roma tomatoes, seeded and drained

1   medium red onion, diced

¼   cup chopped cilantro

¼   cup lime juice

4   ripe avocados, peeled and diced

Salt and pepper to taste

Take the cup of frozen corn and roast under broiler on a cookie sheet; shake pan to caramelize the whole kernels. This process takes only a few minutes and needs some supervision—each oven is different.

In a medium nonreactive bowl, place the beans, corn, tomato, onion, and cilantro, tossing to combine. Drizzle the lime juice over the mixture and toss again. Add the avocado, salt, and pepper and gently toss, careful not to mash avocados.

Transfer the guacamole to a serving bowl and serve with chips.

NOTE: Perfectly ripe avocados make this dish a treat; underripe will taste woody and overripe will mush into the other ingredients, stealing the vibrant colors of this confetti version of guacamole.

In truth, our family has many versions of guacamole, each one usually representing our different trips to California. This one is tasty and certainly stretches the price of an avocado.

Sangrita is a citrus-based chaser for sipping good tequila. In this case, we think it's the perfect spark for ice-cold fresh clams.

Alvaro's Frozen Lime Daiquiri

6   ounces white rum

$\frac{1}{2}$ 8-ounce can frozen limeade

1   egg white

2   cups ice

Lime wedges

Combine rum, frozen limeade, egg white, and ice in a blender.

Blend and pour into wineglass or highball glass. Garnish with lime.

Chilled Clams on the Half Shell with Sangrita

48 fresh littleneck or Manila clams, stored very cold or covered with ice

SANGRITA

$\frac{1}{2}$ cup freshly squeezed orange juice

$\frac{1}{2}$ cup tomato juice

$\frac{1}{4}$ cup fresh lime juice

1   tablespoon Tabasco sauce

Lemon wedges for garnish

Scrub the clams thoroughly with a small brush under cold running water. Briefly soak them in a lukewarm water bath to make it easier to slip the knife between the shells to open.

To shuck a clam, hold it in the palm of your hand and slide a table knife or clam knife (a knife with an easily gripped handle and a thin but not sharp blade) in between the two shells. Slide the knife along the underside of the top shell, separating it from the clam. Pull off the top shell and discard. Slip the knife under the clam to separate it from the shell.

Serve the clams on the half shell on a large platter covered with crushed ice. Mix the liquid sangrita ingredients together and spoon the sangrita over the clams. Garnish with lemon wedges.

Christening Lunch

What do you get when you mix seven Cuban Catholics with the loves of their lives? Answer: Lots of children. With all the weddings it was only a matter of time. Seven of the thirteen grandchildren came in four years! Unlike weddings, where you cannot use your experience organizing your wedding reception more than once (we hope!), baptisms afforded us the chance to create traditions, especially after our third or fourth child.

We always have our favorites made ahead of time so we can eat immediately when we get back from church. The food is a little Cuban, a little Mexican, and a little Argentine; a literal melting pot, all in celebration of another new member of the family.

MENU

MARIQUITAS

SPINACH AND QUESO BLANCO EMPANADAS

CAESAR SALAD

ARROZ CON POLLO

ORANGE ANGEL FOOD CAKE WITH COCONUT ICING

BLOODY MARIAS • BANANA DAIQUIRIS

WINE

ARGENTINE TORRONTES
(SANTA JULIA)

SPANISH JUMILLA
(CASA CASTILLO)

SERVES 12 TO 16

Growing up, this was our potato chip but it didn't come in those fifty-cent deli bags. Try making them yourself and taste the real thing.

Mariquitas

3   cups olive oil

5   green plantains, peeled and thinly sliced

Heat the olive oil in a medium saucepan over medium-high heat until hot but not smoking. In batches, fry the sliced plantain until crisp and golden brown. Using a slotted spoon, remove the plantain to a paper-towel-covered plate to drain. Keep the plate in a warm oven until ready to serve.

Javier's baptism, 1958.

Spinach and Queso Blanco Empanadas

Empanadas are great for leftovers, which is probably why, with seven kids, they showed up at our dinner table once or twice a week.

DOUGH

3 cups all-purpose flour

2 sticks unsalted butter, cubed

$1\frac{1}{2}$ teaspoon salt

$\frac{1}{2}$ cup very cold water

FILLING

2 10-ounce packages frozen chopped spinach, thawed

2 cups crumbled queso blanco cheese

1 tablespoon olive oil

1 small Spanish onion, finely diced

1 clove garlic, minced

1 teaspoon dried oregano

Salt and pepper to taste

1 egg

1 tablespoon water

Preheat oven to 400 degrees. Lightly grease a baking sheet.

In food processor fitted with the metal blade, combine the flour, butter, and salt. Pulse until mixture resembles rough cornmeal. While the motor is running, slowly pour the water through the feed tube until the mixture just forms a ball. Remove dough from bowl, form a ball, and allow it to rest wrapped in plastic; refrigerate for at least 30 minutes.

While the dough is resting, make the filling. In the sink, open the spinach packages and use your hands to squeeze the spinach in batches to remove all the juices, and place in a medium bowl.

Add the queso blanco cheese to the spinach and toss. In a medium sauté pan, heat the olive oil over medium-high heat and sauté onion and garlic until translucent, about 5 minutes. Allow the onion and garlic to cool, then add to the spinach and cheese along with the oregano, salt, and pepper, and toss.

In a small bowl, whisk together the egg and 1 tablespoon water to make an egg wash. Roll dough out on a well-floured surface to a ⅛-inch thickness. Use a 4-inch round cutter to cut out rounds. Using a small pastry brush, brush egg wash completely around the inside edge of the dough and place a tablespoon of filling in the center. Fold the dough over to form a crescent and press edges together to seal. You can either use the back of a fork to seal the edges or press the dough between your index finger, thumb, and middle finger to create a fluted edge.

Brush each empanada with egg wash and place on baking sheet. Bake empanadas for 20–25 minutes or until golden brown.

Serve warm.

Spinach and Queso Blanco Empanadas.

Caesar Salad

3 heads romaine lettuce, shredded, washed, and dried

CROUTONS

$\frac{1}{4}$ cup olive oil

Salt and pepper to taste

$\frac{1}{2}$ loaf day-old French bread, cut into $\frac{1}{2}$-inch cubes

DRESSING

6 anchovy fillets

4 cloves garlic

$\frac{3}{4}$ cup grated Manchego (or Parmesan) cheese

$\frac{1}{2}$ cup fresh lemon juice

2 tablespoons Worcestershire sauce

$1\frac{1}{2}$ tablespoon cracked black pepper

1 tablespoon Dijon mustard

$\frac{1}{2}$ cup olive oil

As we made pilgrimages to California, we became acquainted with this Tijuana classic that is now part of all our repertoires.

Shred and wash the romaine lettuce in very cold water. Pat dry or use a salad spinner to dry thoroughly. Keep the washed lettuce in a large plastic bag with 4 pieces of paper towel until ready to serve.

Combine the ¼ cup olive oil with salt and pepper, add the cubed bread, and toss to coat. Place the bread cubes in a cast-iron skillet over medium-high heat. Use a spatula to toss until bread is toasted golden brown on all sides, about 5 minutes.

While the croutons are baking, prepare the dressing. In a food processor fitted with the metal blade or in a blender, place the anchovy fillets, garlic, ½ cup Parmesan cheese, lemon juice, Worcestershire sauce, pepper, and mustard. Blend on high until smooth. While motor is running, slowly pour ½ cup olive oil in a fine stream into the dressing until it is emulsified. Keep the dressing chilled in the refrigerator until ready to serve.

To serve, place lettuce in salad bowl, pour dressing over it, and toss to coat evenly. Add croutons and toss again. Sprinkle with remaining ¼ cup grated Parmesan cheese and cracked black pepper.

Arroz con Pollo

8   tablespoons olive oil

4   teaspoons hot smoked paprika

3   tablespoons dried oregano

2   tablespoons cumin

1   tablespoon cayenne pepper

1   tablespoon salt

1   tablespoon cracked black pepper

6   whole chicken breasts with skin and bone

4   chorizo sausage, cut into $\frac{1}{2}$-inch pieces

1   large Spanish onion, chopped

5   cloves garlic, minced

2   roasted red peppers, chopped

$\frac{1}{4}$ teaspoon saffron

4   cups long grain rice

4   cups chicken stock

2   12-ounce cans diced tomatoes in juice

4   bay leaves

1   pound frozen peas

Preheat oven to 375 degrees.

Make a rub out of 4 tablespoons of the olive oil and the paprika, oregano, cumin, cayenne pepper, salt, and pepper. Using your hands, rub the chicken with just enough of the mixture to coat it. Set the chicken aside for 10 minutes, allowing the spices to be absorbed.

In a large, heavy Dutch oven, over medium-high heat, brown chorizo in remaining olive oil. Remove the chorizo with a slotted spoon to a plate and lightly brown chicken on both sides, removing to the same plate.

Add the sofrito of onion, garlic, and roasted red peppers and sauté until very soft. Add saffron and rice. Mix for 1 minute to coat rice. Add chicken stock, tomatoes, and bay leaf, stir for 1 minute, and add chicken, chorizo, and peas. Bring to a boil, cover, and bake in oven for 45 minutes.

Reduce oven heat to warm and remove the chicken from the pan, allowing it to cool enough to handle. Using your fingers and a fork, pull or shred the chicken. Return the chicken to the pan and keep covered until ready to serve.

To serve, transfer the chicken and rice to a large bowl and gently toss to combine all the ingredients.

NOTE: A traditional garnish for this dish is artichoke hearts, asparagus spears, and halved hard-boiled eggs.

This dessert combines our
memory of birthdays with
boxed cake and a love of
citrus and coconut.

We are Cuban, after all.

Orange Angel Food Cake with Coconut Icing

CAKE

1   cup cake flour (not self-rising)

$1\frac{1}{4}$ cup superfine sugar

$\frac{1}{2}$ teaspoon salt

11 egg whites

$\frac{1}{2}$ teaspoon cream of tartar

1   teaspoon orange extract

2   tablespoons orange zest

FROSTING

1   cup sugar

2   large egg whites

$\frac{1}{4}$ cup water

1   tablespoon light corn syrup

1   teaspoon coconut extract

2   cups shredded coconut

Preheat oven to 350 degrees.

In a large bowl, sift the cake flour, ½ cup sugar, and salt 3 times. In the bowl of an electric mixer, beat the egg whites on high for 1 minute. Add the cream of tartar and beat until soft peaks just start to form. Add the orange extract and slowly add the rest of the sugar; continue beating until stiff peaks form.

Fold half the flour-and-sugar mixture into the egg whites with a wire whisk until incorporated, then fold in the second half. Spoon the batter into an angel-food-cake pan and bake in the center of the oven for 45 minutes, until a knife inserted into the center comes out clean.

To help the cake maintain its shape, invert the cake pan onto a wine bottle and allow cake to cool upside down for at least an hour. While the cake is cooling, prepare the frosting. In a large heat-proof bowl, mix the sugar, egg whites, water, corn syrup, and coconut extract. Whisk together over a saucepan of simmering water for 2 minutes. Using a hand-held electric mixer, beat the syrup on high for 7–10 minutes until the sugar is completely dissolved and the frosting is fluffy. Remove the icing from the simmering water and continue beating until the frosting is cool.

Using a rubber spatula, fold in 1 cup of the shredded coconut. Ice the cake and sprinkle remaining coconut over it.

Bloody Maria

2	ounces tequila
5	ounces tomato juice
3	dashes Worcestershire sauce
$\frac{1}{2}$	lemon, juiced
3	dashes Tabasco sauce
Ice	

Combine ingredients over ice and quickly pour from one glass into another and back to mix.

NOTE: You can dust rim of glass with celery salt for a special touch.

VARIATION: Substitute beef bouillon for tomato juice to create a Bull Shot.

Banana Daiquiri

2	ounces white rum
1	ounce crème de banane
1	lime, juiced
$\frac{1}{2}$	banana, ripe
Crushed ice	
Fresh mint	

Combine first five ingredients in blender and blend. Pour into wineglass or highball glass and garnish with mint.

Midweek Dinner

Cuba has a wonderful climate. Thanks to the trade winds, temperatures that record oppressive heat feel merely very warm. Cubans will tell you it is a perfect climate for a beautiful country. They compare it favorably to San Diego's weather. They also forget to mention the humidity. That great meteorological force, which makes Cuba an ideal place to grow tobacco, is ever present. You cannot have it all.

In fact, sometimes you cannot have it at all. February in New York provides the stark contrast. Damp and cold with snow, sleet, or freezing rain—or all three—define the average daily weather for that month. We attempt to get through the longest shortest month with dinners at each other's homes. The food: simple, tasty, and homemade.

MENU

PLANTAIN SOUP WITH ROMESCO SAUCE

WATERCRESS, AVOCADO, AND ONION SALAD

CHICKEN FRICASSEE

ROASTED PURPLE PERUVIAN POTATOES

PINEAPPLE CUPCAKES

TROPICAL FRUIT MARGARITAS

WINE
CHILEAN SAUVIGNON BLANC
(VERAMONTE)

CHILEAN CARMENERE
(CALINA)

SERVES 6 TO 8

Opposite: Plantain Soup with Romesco Sauce.

Plantain Soup with Romesco Sauce

SOUP

6   tablespoons olive oil

3   cloves garlic, minced

1   large Spanish onion, minced

1   carrot, finely diced

1   stalk celery, finely diced

1   roasted green bell pepper, finely chopped

5   green plantains, peeled and sliced in half lengthwise

8   cups chicken stock

Salt and pepper

SAUCE

4   plum tomatoes, sliced in half lengthwise

8   cloves garlic, peeled

18 whole almonds, blanched

$\frac{1}{2}$ cup plus 1 tablespoon olive oil

4   tablespoons red wine vinegar

2   slices white bread, toasted and cut in quarters

$\frac{1}{2}$ cup roasted red pepper

$\frac{1}{2}$ teaspoon salt

$\frac{1}{2}$ teaspoon cracked black pepper

$\frac{1}{4}$ teaspoon red pepper flakes

To make the soup: In a large, heavy stockpot heat 4 tablespoons of olive oil and sauté the garlic, onion, carrot, celery, and roasted green pepper for 10 minutes until the vegetables are translucent.

While the vegetables are sautéing, heat the remaining 2 tablespoons of olive oil and sauté the plantains until they are golden.

Add the chicken stock to the sautéed vegetables and stir for 1 minute. Add the sautéed plantains. Bring the mixture just to a boil and reduce the heat to low. Allow the soup to simmer for about 40 minutes or until it is reduced by one quarter.

Complete the soup by pureeing in batches, in a blender or with a hand-held blender. Add salt and pepper to taste. Serve hot with a healthy dollop of romesco sauce.

Amy and Mateo.

To make the sauce: Preheat oven to 400 degrees.

Place tomatoes and garlic on a lightly oiled baking sheet and roast for 25 minutes.

In a nonstick skillet, toast almonds in 1 tablespoon of olive oil until just golden. Nuts will cook quickly and require constant attention.

In a blender or a food processor fitted with the metal blade, place the garlic, tomatoes, almonds, remaining olive oil, vinegar, toast, roasted red pepper, salt, black pepper, and pepper flakes. Blend on high or pulse food processor, scraping down the sides of the container with a rubber spatula, until smooth.

Serve at room temperature. Romesco sauce can be kept refrigerated for 1 week in an airtight container.

MAKES 2 CUPS

Watercress, Avocado, and Onion Salad

$^2/_3$ cup olive oil

$^1/_4$ cup white wine vinegar

$^1/_4$ cup orange juice

4 cloves garlic, minced

1 tablespoon fresh lime juice

Salt and pepper to taste

3 bunches watercress, washed and dried

2 avocados, peeled and sliced

1 small red onion, sliced

Combine olive oil, vinegar, orange juice, garlic, lime juice, salt, and pepper in a small jar, cover with lid, and shake vigorously until the vinaigrette is emulsified, about 30 seconds. Taste and adjust seasoning.

Divide watercress among 8 salad plates, top with avocado and onion slices, and drizzle with vinaigrette. Serve immediately.

A great family meal, this dish takes the simplest components and dresses up chicken. Although we have this several times a month, it works for a dinner party too.

Chicken Fricassee

4   chicken breasts, with skin and bone
4   chicken thighs, with skin and bone
Salt and pepper to taste
$\frac{1}{2}$ cup olive oil
2   large Spanish onions, peeled and chopped
2   whole heads garlic, peeled and sliced
$\frac{1}{2}$ cup dry white wine
3   cups chicken stock reduced to half
Juice of 2 lemons
2   teaspoons dried oregano
1   $5\frac{1}{2}$-ounce jar Spanish green olives
1   medium Spanish onion, thinly sliced into rings
1   lemon, thinly sliced into rounds

Preheat oven to 350 degrees.

Wash chicken under cold water and pat dry. Season with salt and pepper. Heat ¼ cup oil in a large Dutch oven over medium-high heat and brown chicken on both sides. Remove chicken to a plate and set aside.

Add remaining olive oil to Dutch oven, add chopped onions, and sauté until translucent, about 5 minutes. Add garlic and sauté for an additional 2 minutes. Add wine and cook for 1 minute, then add chicken stock, lemon juice, and oregano. Return chicken pieces to pan.

Layer olives, onion rings, and lemon slices over the chicken, cover, and place in oven. Cook for 50–60 minutes until the juice of the chicken runs clear.

Arrange chicken with onion, lemon, and olives on a heatproof serving platter and keep warm in oven.

Reduce liquid by one quarter over medium-high heat for sauce. Taste and adjust seasoning. Pour over the chicken.

The first dish I ever cooked for a date was this potato dish, and it was a winner. Any potato will do, but these purple Peruvian potatoes have a sweetness all their own.

Roasted Purple Peruvian Potatoes

1½ pound small purple Peruvian potatoes, washed and quartered

7 cloves garlic, minced

3 sprigs rosemary, finely chopped

3 tablespoons olive oil

Salt and pepper to taste

Preheat oven to 350 degrees.

In a large mixing bowl, combine the potatoes, garlic, rosemary, olive oil, salt, and pepper. Mix potatoes until evenly coated and place in a roasting pan. Roast for 60 minutes until browned and soft when pricked with a fork.

The kids always clean their plates to get to these. We served them along with birthday cakes growing up.

Pineapple Cupcakes

BATTER

1¼ cup all-purpose flour

¾ teaspoon baking powder

¼ teaspoon baking soda

Pinch salt

1 20-ounce can crushed pineapple

6 tablespoons unsalted butter, softened

¾ cup sugar

2 eggs

½ teaspoon vanilla

1 teaspoon pineapple extract

½ cup whole milk

FROSTING

1 cup confectioners' sugar, sifted if necessary

2 tablespoons unsalted butter, softened

2–3 tablespoons milk

½ teaspoon vanilla

Pinch salt

Food coloring, optional

Preheat oven to 350 degrees. Line a cupcake tin with paper liners.

Whisk together the flour, baking powder, baking soda, and salt. In a fine sieve, drain the crushed pineapple, using your hands to press out as much liquid as possible. Set aside.

Beat the butter and sugar with an electric mixer at medium-high speed for 3–4 minutes until light and creamy. Mix in the eggs, one at a time. Add the vanilla and pineapple extract, beating just until mixed.

With the mixer on low speed, add the dry ingredients in three parts, alternating with the milk. Beat just until the flour is incorporated. Gently stir in 1 cup crushed pineapple.

Spoon enough batter to fill each cup ¾ full and bake the cupcakes for 20–25 minutes, until a knife inserted into the center comes out clean.

Remove the cupcake tin from the oven and let it cool for 5 minutes. Remove the cupcakes from the tin and let them cool, still in their liners, set on metal racks.

While the cupcakes are cooling, prepare the frosting. Beat together the confectioners' sugar and butter with an electric mixer set on medium speed until smooth.

With the mixer running, add 2 tablespoons of milk, the vanilla, and a pinch of salt. Beat until smooth. If the frosting seems thin, let it sit for a few minutes. It may thicken up. Or set it over a bowl of ice water and whisk to thicken. If still too thin, add more sugar.

Use immediately.

MAKES 12 CUPCAKES

Tropical Fruit Margarita

2   ounces silver or gold tequila
1   ounce Cointreau
1   ounce lime juice
2   ounces tropical fruit juice
     (mango or papaya)
Fresh mint or sliced fruit
Ice

Combine liquid ingredients with ice in a shaker and shake. Strain into a chilled martini glass or pour over ice in a highball glass and garnish with a sprig of mint or slice of fruit.

To make this drink frozen, double the ingredients and pour into a blender full of ice. Blend. Fresh, frozen, or canned fruit may be added for more flavor and richness.

Javier's birthday, 1965.

Easter Lunch

We welcome spring back with what is the first trip of the New Year to Bridgehampton, New York. The three Saralegui houses provide plenty of worthy hiding places for eggs. The adults do not compete for the candy, but with Lent over, this meal is a feast.

The beauty of Bridgehampton in the spring cannot be overstated. Plant shoots are popping up all over the garden; indeed, green is the theme of the day.

The children collecting eggs on Easter morning.

Opposite: Rack of Lamb with Mint Pesto.

MENU

GARLIC-LIME SOUP

AMY'S ENCHILADAS

TOMATILLO RELISH

RACK OF LAMB WITH MINT PESTO

GREEN RICE

TATI'S NATILLA

WHITE SANGRIA

WINE
ARGENTINE MALBEC
(ALTOS LAS HORMIGAS)

SERVES 8

Garlic-Lime Soup

CHICKEN STOCK

1   4–5-pound whole chicken, rinsed

16 cups cold water

1   onion, cut in half

1   carrot

1   celery stalk

2   roasted green bell peppers

2   large roasted tomatoes

1   bay leaf

SOUP

¼   cup olive oil

¼   medium Spanish onion, chopped

20 cloves garlic, sliced

5   limes, 4 juiced and 1 thinly sliced

8   cups chicken stock

Salt and pepper to taste

3   small radishes, thinly sliced

1   avocado, peeled, pitted, and diced

To make the stock: Place the whole chicken in a large heavy stockpot and cover with cold water. Bring the water to a boil and reduce to a simmer for 30 minutes and skim off residue. Add the onion, carrot, celery, peppers, tomatoes, and bay leaf. Continue simmering for approximately 3 hours, adding water if needed to keep the chicken covered.

   Strain the stock into a clean bowl.

MAKES 8 CUPS

   To make the soup: In a heavy stockpot, heat the olive oil over medium heat until hot but not smoking, add the onion, and cook until translucent, about 3 minutes. Add the sliced cloves of garlic and sauté for 1–2 minutes.

Isabel.

Add the lime juice and stir to reduce for 1 minute, then add the chicken stock. Bring the soup to a boil, then reduce to low and simmer for 15 minutes until reduced slightly.

In a blender or using a hand-held blender, puree the soup and return to pot. Heat the soup until just hot. Taste and adjust seasoning with salt and pepper.

To serve, float a thin slice of lime with 2 radish slices and a few chunks of avocado in each bowl for garnish.

This is a version of the classic Tex-Mex crowd pleaser known as enchiladas Suizas. I didn't know about them until I married a Texan. My wife, Amy, has favorite versions of the dish all over Austin, but this one is inspired by an Austin treasure, chef Miguel Ravago.

Amy's Enchiladas

3   medium chicken breasts, bone-in

6   medium tomatillos, husked

Vegetable oil

1   4-ounce can chopped green chilies

4   cloves garlic, sliced

½   cup (1 stick) unsalted butter

¼   cup all-purpose flour

1¾ cup sour cream

Salt and pepper to taste

1   medium Spanish onion, finely chopped

2   cups shredded Monterey Jack cheese

24 white corn tortillas

Preheat oven to 350 degrees.

To prepare the chicken breasts, place them in a large stockpot and cover with cold water by 1 inch. Bring the water to a boil, reduce the heat to medium-low, and allow the chicken to simmer until the meat is cooked through, about 30 minutes. Using tongs, remove the chicken from the pot and allow it to cool enough to handle. Reserve 2 cups of chicken water.

Using your fingers and a fork, pull the chicken meat from the bone, shred, and dice with a sharp knife.

To prepare the tomatillo salsa, heat a cast-iron skillet on high until hot and add the tomatillos. Cook until they are blistered on all sides. Remove from pan. Add 2 tablespoons vegetable oil to the pan and add green chilies and sliced garlic. Sauté for 1 minute.

In a food processor fitted with the metal blade or in a blender, mix the tomatillos with the garlic and green chilies, processing until smooth. Use a rubber spatula to scrape down the sides of the bowl.

To make the green sauce, melt the butter in a large skillet over medium heat. Whisk in the flour until smooth. Add the reserved 2 cups chicken broth, stirring constantly until incorporated. Add 1 cup sour cream and 8 tablespoons of the tomatillo salsa, whisking until combined thoroughly. Season with salt and pepper to taste and set aside.

To make the filling, combine the onion, 1 cup Jack cheese, remaining $\frac{3}{4}$ cup sour cream, shredded chicken, salt, and pepper in a large bowl and set aside.

In the cast-iron skillet used for the tomatillos, heat $\frac{1}{8}$ inch of vegetable oil over medium-high heat until hot. Using tongs, place each tortilla, one at a time, in the oil and allow it to fry until just softened, then turn over to second side, approximately 5 seconds a side. Remove from pan and layer tortillas with paper towels. Allow them to cool enough to handle.

To assemble the enchiladas, spread half the green sauce over the bottom of a 10 x 15 x 3–inch casserole dish. Spread each tortilla with 2 tablespoons of the filling across the center. Roll up the tortillas and place them seam side down in the casserole dish.

Cover the enchiladas with the remaining green sauce and sprinkle with remaining Jack cheese. Bake for 30 minutes or until bubbling hot. Serve with Tomatillo Relish.

Tomatillo Relish

2   tomatillos, diced

1   jalapeño, seeded and minced

$\frac{1}{4}$ Spanish onion, diced

$\frac{1}{4}$ avocado, peeled, seeded, and diced

Juice of 1 lime

Salt and pepper to taste

In a nonreactive bowl, mix the tomatillos and jalapeño together. Add the onion, avocado, lime juice, salt, and pepper and mix to combine.

Serve at room temperature. Relish can be made 1 day in advance.

MAKES ROUGHLY $\frac{1}{2}$ CUP

Mint, lime, and garlic—
we figure if these basic
ingredients are good enough
for a mojito—the Cuban
national cocktail—they
should be great for lamb.

Rack of Lamb
with Mint Pesto

PESTO

8 cloves garlic

2 bunches mint leaves

2 bunches flat-leaf parsley leaves

1 cup olive oil

Salt and pepper to taste

MARINADE

$\frac{1}{3}$ cup mint pesto

Juice of 2 limes

$1\frac{1}{2}$ cup olive oil

LAMB

3 tablespoons olive oil or more

4 racks of lamb (8 ribs each, about $1\frac{1}{2}$ pounds each), French-cut

12 small cloves garlic

To make the pesto, place the garlic, mint, parsley, 1 cup olive oil, salt, and pepper in a food processor fitted with the metal blade. Pulse until mixture is a thick sauce, using a spatula to scrape down the sides. Makes 2 cups.

To make the marinade, mix $\frac{1}{3}$ cup pesto, lime juice, and $1\frac{1}{2}$ cup olive oil together with a fork in a nonreactive bowl.

Using a sharp knife, cut each rack of lamb in half, leaving 4 ribs to each half. Make a small incision between each rib and place one small clove of garlic in each incision. Place the racks in a glass dish and pour the marinade over the racks. Use your fingers to smear the marinade over the entire surface of each rack. Cover with plastic wrap and allow the lamb to marinate for at least 1 hour, up to 3 hours.

In a large skillet, heat 3 tablespoons olive oil over medium-high heat until hot but not smoking. Lightly brown on all sides 2 pieces of lamb at a time. This should take about one minute for each batch. Add more olive oil if necessary to keep lamb from sticking to pan. Place the pieces as browned into a large, shallow roasting pan, meat side up.

Roast the lamb in the center of the oven for 20–25 minutes until a thermometer inserted into the center of each piece registers 135 degrees for medium-rare. Transfer each piece to a cutting board and allow to rest, loosely covered with aluminum foil, for 10 minutes.

Slice each piece into 4 individual lamb chops and serve with a healthy spoonful of mint pesto drizzled over the chops.

NOTE: For this recipe, ask your butcher to French-cut the racks of lamb for you.

Green Rice

4   cups water
2   cups long-grain rice
2   cups parsley leaves
2   cups cilantro leaves
3   scallions, trimmed
1   roasted poblano pepper, seeded
3   tablespoons butter (optional)
Salt and pepper

In a heavy medium pot with lid, bring 3 cups of water to a boil, add rice, cover, and reduce heat to low. Allow the rice to simmer for 15 minutes or until the water is absorbed.

While rice is cooking, puree the parsley, cilantro, scallions, and poblano pepper in the remaining 1 cup of water in a blender or food processor fitted with the metal blade. Check the rice to see if cooking water has been absorbed and stir in the herb puree, cover, and allow the rice to absorb the herb water for another 5–8 minutes.

Transfer rice to a bowl, add the butter if desired, and gently toss to melt it; add salt and pepper to taste.

Christian.

Tati's Natilla

8   egg yolks

3   cups whole milk

1½ cup granulated sugar

1   cinnamon stick

1   teaspoon vanilla

4   tablespoons cornstarch

¼   cup water

Preheat oven to 350 degrees.

In a large bowl, whisk together the egg yolks, milk, sugar, cinnamon stick, and vanilla. Dissolve the cornstarch in the water and whisk into the milk mixture. In a heavy medium saucepan, heat mixture over medium heat, stirring constantly for 20 minutes until it starts to thicken and coats the back of a spoon.

Remove the mixture from heat and immediately pour into an ovenproof bowl or individual cups. Place the custard bowl or cups in a shallow roasting pan and fill the roasting pan three quarters full with warm water, or halfway up the individual cups. Bake for 40–50 minutes until custard is set. Remove from oven and allow to cool to room temperature, cover with plastic, and refrigerate.

Opposite: Annick.

We ate this custard dessert more often than any other, probably because after we devastated all the ice cream and Pop Tarts in the house all we had left was milk, eggs, and sugar.

White Sangria

3   bottles of white wine, Pinot Blanc
    or Pinot Gris

1   quart apple juice

1   quart white grape juice

1   pint lemon juice

1   pint pineapple juice

2   apples, cored and sliced

1   bunch grapes, sliced

1   melon, ripe and cubed or balled

Fresh mint

Soda water (optional)

Combine all ingredients except mint and soda water in a pitcher and chill. Pour over ice, garnish with mint sprig, and top with splash of soda water if desired.

Three-Day-Weekend Dinner

These summer weekends allow us extra time to catch up. Sunday we luxuriate by the pool and skip our workouts. Then, we make a special dinner. Lobster, summer vegetables, margaritas, and the company make these meals a favorite. We repeat this meal often from May to September because of the fresh summer flavors that are New England with a little cha cha cha.

MENU

STEAMED LOBSTER WITH LIME, TOMATILLO, AND JALAPEÑO BEURRE BLANC

MELON BALL AND QUESO BLANCO SALAD

GRILLED SUMMER VEGETABLES WITH JALAPEÑO MINT OIL

PEACH AND MANGO COBBLER

CLASSIC MARGARITAS

WINE
SPANISH CAVA
(BODEGAS EL CEP MARQUES DE GELIDA)

SERVES 6

Butter and lobster fit hand in glove. A good friend taught me this variation, and every summer when we gather, sometimes for a birthday, this dish is the first request.

Steamed Lobster with Lime, Tomatillo, and Jalapeño Beurre Blanc

2   lemons, sliced into quarters

1   packet commercial lobster/crab boil (such as Zatarain's)

6   1½–2-pound live lobsters

4   fresh tomatillos, coarsely chopped

1   jalapeño, ribs and seeds removed, chopped

2   tablespoons olive oil

1   cup white wine

1   cup butter (2 sticks) plus 2 tablespoons, cut into small pieces

2   tablespoons lime juice

1   bunch fresh cilantro, chopped

Fill 2 large stockpots three quarters full with water. Add 2 quarters of lemon and half the seafood seasoning to each pot. Bring the water to a rapid boil over high heat.

Plunge lobsters headfirst into boiling water, 3 per pot, making sure that water completely covers each lobster to ensure even cooking. You may need to boil the lobsters in batches if your pots are not large enough to accommodate all of them at once.

Boil the lobsters for approximately 12 minutes, or until they turn bright red. Carefully remove from the water with tongs and set aside.

In a medium saucepan, sauté chopped tomatillos and jalapeños in 2 tablespoons olive oil for approximately 3 minutes. Add white wine and cook for an additional 5 minutes. Begin adding pieces of butter, one at a time, letting each piece melt, until fully incorporated. Remove from heat and finish by stirring in lime juice and chopped cilantro.

Place lime-tomatillo sauce in small bowls for dipping. Use lobster crackers and picks to break lobster shells and tails. Use a lobster pick to pull meat from the shells and dip into the sauce.

Melon Ball and
Queso Blanco Salad

1   ripe honeydew melon

1   ripe cantaloupe

1/4   ripe seedless watermelon

1/2   cup grated queso blanco cheese

1   lime

2   tablespoons chopped mint

Using two or three different-size melon ballers, scoop out the melons into a large bowl. Sprinkle the grated cheese and cut and squeeze the lime over the melon balls. Toss to mix well and serve chilled with a sprinkle of mint at the last moment.

This salad is refreshing and pretty. When my friend and talented chef John Pecore served it to me, all I could wonder was, why didn't I think of this? Now we serve it all the time. This is one dish worth buying an assortment of melon ballers for.

Classic Margarita

2$\frac{1}{2}$ ounces gold tequila

1   ounce triple sec or Cointreau
       or Grand Marnier

1   ounce fresh lime juice

Kosher salt

Ice

When I was a bartender, margaritas were my specialty. This drink is made wrong more often than not. Foreign citrus mixers like Rose's lime juice and sour mix have no place in a margarita. The original margarita was made of half and half silver tequila and Mexican limes. These limes, like key limes, are sweet. To create a similar balance, we use everyday sour limes and balance the sour with an orange-based liqueur such as triple sec, Cointreau, or Grand Marnier; these liqueurs are very sweet. Depending how you like your margarita—tart or sweet, I prefer tart margaritas—the balance of the lime juice with the liqueur will deliver the proper blend. To add the aforementioned citrus mixers creates a redundant and cloyingly sweet drink. Did I mention we take our cocktails seriously?

Combine ingredients in mixing glass and shake. Strain into a (salted or not) wineglass or highball glass, over fresh ice. Garnish with lime.

Grilled Summer Vegetables with Jalapeño Mint Oil

SUMMER VEGETABLES

2   medium eggplants, sliced in $\frac{1}{2}$-inch rounds and "sweated"

3   tablespoons sea salt

2   medium zucchinis, cut in $\frac{1}{4}$-inch slices lengthwise

2   medium summer squash, cut in $\frac{1}{4}$-inch slices lengthwise

1   cup olive oil

JALAPEÑO MINT OIL

1   cup olive oil

2   tablespoons chopped mint, plus sprigs for garnish

1   jalapeño pepper, ribs and seeds removed, chopped

Salt to taste

Mint leaves

Place sliced eggplant in bowl and sprinkle with salt. Toss and let sweat for 15 minutes. Drain.

In a large bowl, toss all the vegetables with $\frac{1}{2}$ cup olive oil. On a medium-hot grill, grill the vegetables until tender, approximately 3 to 5 minutes a side, brushing with olive oil as needed. Remove the vegetables as they become fully cooked to a platter, arranging them in a fan shape.

To make the flavored oil, heat the olive oil in a saucepan until hot but not smoking. Add the mint and jalapeño and remove the saucepan from heat. Allow the olive oil to cool completely, then strain through a fine sieve to remove the mint and jalapeño.

To serve, drizzle the vegetables with flavored oil and salt to taste. Garnish with mint leaves.

Peach and Mango Cobbler

CRUST

2½ cups all-purpose flour

1   teaspoon granulated sugar

1   teaspoon salt

1   cup (2 sticks) unsalted butter, chilled, cut into pieces

6–8 tablespoons water

FILLING

6   ripe peaches, peeled and sliced, or 2 1-pound cans
       or 4 cups frozen

6   ripe mangoes, peeled and sliced, or 2 1-pound cans
       or 4 cups frozen

¼   cup light brown sugar

2   tablespoons dark rum (Meyer's)

¼   cup (½ stick) unsalted butter, cut into small cubes

To make the dough, whisk together the flour, sugar, and salt. Add the butter, and using your fingers, 2 knives, or a pastry blender, blend the butter into the flour mixture until it resembles coarse meal. Add the water 1 tablespoon at a time until dough just comes together when pressed between two fingers.

Form the dough into a ball, wrap, and refrigerate for at least 30 minutes or overnight.

Preheat oven to 375 degrees. Butter a 13 x 9 x 2-inch baking dish.

Place the sliced fruit in a buttered baking dish and mix to distribute evenly. Sprinkle with three-fourths of the sugar and the rum and dot with butter. Roll out the pie dough on a floured surface, making it large enough to cover the pan. Place the dough on top and press around the edges to seal. Using a knife, slice a few holes through the dough to allow steam to escape. Sprinkle the dough with the remaining sugar and bake for 45 minutes until the filling is bubbling hot.

Serve the cobbler hot, warm, or chilled with vanilla ice cream or whipped cream.

When our grandmother Gui Gui came to the United States she settled in South Carolina. Our uncle Eddy was training to fight in the Bay of Pigs invasion and he was stationed at Fort Jackson in Columbia. The beautiful peaches in that part of the country caught her eye, and she put them to delicious use in this cobbler recipe.

Softball Mixed-Grill Picnic

Our grandfather's life is a Basque/Cuban Horatio Alger story. Abuelo Saralegui was born in the Basque country and orphaned at age one. He later built one of the largest trading and publishing companies in Latin America. He purchased a partial ownership of the Havana Sugar Kings, enjoying the closest thing Cuba had to a major league club.

We all share some of Abuelo's characteristics and passions. We are all competitive, love baseball, and love to eat. When you put all three together, you finish with a competitive game, family statistics, and full stomachs. We review the key plays in our post-game discussion, often milking the most dramatic ones we made.

MENU

CHIMICHURRI-MARINATED FLANK STEAK SANDWICHES WITH AVOCADO

STUFFED JALAPEÑO AND JACK BURGER

CHARRED TOMATO RELISH

GUAVA-BASTED RIBS

PINEAPPLE AND JICAMA SLAW

LEMON SORBET WITH AÑEJO TEQUILA

MICHOLADAS

WINE
MEXICAN CABERNET
(MONTE XANIC CABERNET-MERLOT)

*Opposite: Chimichurri-Marinated Flank
Steak Sandwiches with Avocado.*

SERVES 10 TO 12

Although it may be unpatriotic in Cuba to say that mojo is not your favorite sauce, the Argentine chimichurri certainly is a strong runner-up.

Chimichurri-Marinated Flank Steak Sandwiches with Avocado

10 cloves garlic

1 cup fresh oregano

1 cup parsley

$\frac{1}{2}$ cup olive oil

$\frac{1}{4}$ cup champagne vinegar or white wine vinegar

Juice of $\frac{1}{2}$ lime

Teaspoon red pepper flakes

Salt and pepper

1 2-pound flank steak

2 avocados, peeled and pitted

1 loaf thick-crust peasant bread, cut into $\frac{1}{2}$-inch slices

In a food processor fitted with a metal blade, puree the garlic, oregano, parsley, olive oil, vinegar, lime juice, red pepper flakes, salt, and pepper. Place the flank steak in a sealable plastic bag and pour the chimichurri marinade over the steak. Marinate for a minimum of 4 hours or overnight.

On a hot grill, grill the flank steak for 6–7 minutes on each side until the meat is cooked to medium-rare. Let the flank steak rest for 5 minutes before slicing thinly across the grain.

Mash the avocados in a nonreactive bowl and toast the bread on the grill. To make the sandwiches, spread avocado on one slice of bread for each sandwich, add sliced flank steak, drizzle with fresh chimichurri, season with salt and pepper, and top with the second slice of bread.

Stuffed Jalapeño and Jack Burger

4–5 pounds ground beef

1 tablespoon dried oregano

1 tablespoon garlic pepper

1 teaspoon salt

½ pound Monterey Jack cheese, grated

Sliced canned jalapeños

3 roasted green peppers, quartered

Ketchup or Charred Tomato Relish (recipe on page 68)

Preheat grill on medium-high heat.

In a large bowl, mix ground beef with oregano, garlic pepper, and salt. Divide the meat evenly to make 8–10 burgers. Form the meat into patties, and split each patty through the center into 2 patties. Flatten the patties and sprinkle one of each half with 2–3 tablespoons of the grated cheese and slices of jalapeño. Place the other half patty on top and pinch the edges together to seal in the cheese and jalapeño peppers.

On a hot grill, grill the burgers for 5 minutes on each side or until desired doneness is reached. Serve on toasted bun with a slice of roasted green pepper and ketchup or Charred Tomato Relish.

These stuffed burgers are a south Texas standard. They're great on the grill.

BBQ sauce is tangy and often sweet. Here the guava adds a unique sweetness and pungency and brings the whole meal back to Cuba and *béisbol*.

   This is a 3-stage recipe requiring the better part of 4 hours. This recipe could be broken down into 2 days. Ask any southerner, good ribs are worth the work.

Guava-Basted Ribs

5–6 pounds pork ribs, individually sliced

RIB MARINADE

$1\frac{1}{2}$ cup olive oil

1   head garlic

1   tablespoon dried oregano

2   teaspoons salt

2   teaspoons cracked black pepper

BRAISING LIQUID

2   quarts (8 cups) chicken stock

4   garlic cloves, minced

1   large Spanish onion, diced

1   carrot, diced

1   celery stalk, diced

1   teaspoon dried oregano

4   bay leaves

GUAVA BBQ SAUCE

6   tablespoons olive oil

3   medium onions, chopped

3   roasted red peppers, or one 12-ounce jar

$2\frac{1}{2}$ cups guava jelly

1   cup red wine vinegar

$\frac{1}{2}$ cup plus 1 tablespoon molasses

6   jalapeños, seeded and chopped

1   tablespoon salt

1   teaspoon allspice

Place all the marinade ingredients in a food processor fitted with the metal blade and puree. Place the ribs in a large nonreactive container and pour the marinade over them to cover. Cover the container and allow the ribs to marinate in the refrigerator for 1 hour.

   Preheat oven to 300 degrees. While the ribs are marinating, make the braising liquid. Combine all the braising ingredients in a large bowl and set aside. When the ribs have finished marinating, place them in a large Dutch oven with the liquid and braise, covered, for 2 hours.

While the ribs are braising, make the barbecue sauce. In a medium saucepan, sauté the onion and red pepper in olive oil over medium-high heat for 3 minutes. Stir in the remaining ingredients and simmer over low heat for 40 minutes. Allow the mixture to cool slightly, then puree in a food processor fitted with the metal blade.

Turn oven up to 350 degrees and place the ribs on a baking sheet. Pour the guava barbecue sauce over the ribs and bake for 15 minutes.

NOTE: If you prefer, grill for 5 minutes on each side and finish in a 350-degree oven for 10 minutes—molasses tends to burn on the grill.

Charred Tomato Relish

3   ripe plum tomatoes, halved lengthwise

1   medium Spanish onion, thickly sliced

1   jalapeño pepper, sliced in half and seeded

2   tablespoons minced garlic

1   tablespoon chopped parsley

1   tablespoon chopped cilantro

Salt and pepper

Heat a grill or grill pan until hot. Preheat oven to 300 degrees. Grill the tomatoes, onion, and jalapeño until they are dark brown in color; remove from heat immediately.

Place the grilled tomatoes, onion, and jalapeño in a heat-proof bowl and add the garlic, parsley, and cilantro. Mix to combine and bake for 1 hour until the mixture is dark in color. Remove the relish from the oven and let it cool to room temperature.

Once cooled, place the relish in the bowl of food processor fitted with the metal blade and pulse 3 to 4 times until it resembles a rough chop, or use a sharp knife to chop the mixture into a relish. Relish can be made 2 days in advance.

MAKES ROUGHLY 1/2 CUP

Pineapple and Jicama Slaw

1   ripe pineapple, peeled, core removed, and diced

1   medium jicama, peeled and julienned

4   carrots, peeled and julienned

1   cup olive oil

Juice of 1$\frac{1}{2}$ limes

$\frac{1}{4}$ cup white wine or champagne vinegar

$\frac{1}{3}$ cup pineapple juice

1   teaspoon ground cumin

1   teaspoon red pepper flakes

Salt and pepper to taste

$\frac{1}{4}$ cup shredded fresh basil (chiffonade)

$\frac{1}{4}$ cup shredded fresh mint

Cut the jicama into spears small enough to fit into the feed tube of a food processor. Use the fine-shred or julienne disk for both the jicama and carrot, or cut both with a sharp knife. Drain the juice from the pineapple into a glass jar or plastic container with lid.

In a large nonreactive bowl, combine the jicama and pineapple and set aside.

To make the dressing, combine the olive oil, lime juice, vinegar, pineapple juice, cumin, red pepper flakes, salt, and pepper. Tightly close the lid and shake vigorously until the vinaigrette is emulsified, about 30 seconds. Pour the dressing over the pineapple, jicama, and carrots and toss to coat evenly.

Add the basil and mint, gently tossing to blend. Taste and adjust seasoning with salt and pepper.

Lemon Sorbet and Añejo Tequila

Finish the meal by serving your favorite lemon sorbet, with a drizzle of añejo tequila and a side shot.

Micholada

1 bottle of amber beer, Negra Modelo

Juice of $\frac{1}{2}$ lemon

Tabasco sauce

Ice

Combine ingredients in highball glass full of ice. On a hot day it'll cure what ails you.

If you have a taste for añejo tequila, and we do, this will certainly cleanse your palate.

Fourth of July Latin Clambake

The Fourth of July weekend combines two occasions to celebrate: the founding of our adopted country and my birthday. We make an effort for a late afternoon sunset party on the beach. Flavors from our mom's and our grandmother Amalita's cooking highlight the meal. If you squint very hard after a few Cuba Libres, you can transport yourself to the beach at Varadero, Cuba. There is always plenty of food and drink for anybody who drops by.

MENU

GRILLED OYSTERS WITH CHIMICHURRI

MAMI'S GAZPACHO

GRILLED MAHIMAHI STEAKS WITH
JALAPEÑO-MINT-COMPOUND BUTTER

CORN ON THE COALS WITH LIME AND CAYENNE

GRILLED PINEAPPLE WITH
SUMMER BERRY COMPOTE

CUBA LIBRES

SALT-RIMMED BEER WITH LIME

WINE
ARGENTINE PINOT GRIGIO
(GRAFFIGNA)

PORTUGUESE ALENTEJO
(JP VINHOS TINTO)

*Opposite: Grilled Oysters
with Chimichurri.*

SERVES 8 TO 10

This simple combination works and is a great way to introduce newcomers to oysters. It has won over even the pickiest Saralegui.

Grilled Oysters with Chimichurri

10 cloves garlic

$\frac{1}{4}$ cup fresh oregano

1   cup parsley

$\frac{1}{2}$ cup olive oil

$\frac{1}{4}$ cup champagne vinegar

Juice of $\frac{1}{2}$ lime

1   teaspoon red pepper flakes

Salt and pepper to taste

3   dozen fresh oysters

To make the chimichurri sauce, puree the garlic, oregano, parsley, olive oil, vinegar, lime juice, red pepper flakes, salt, and pepper in a food processor fitted with the metal blade. The chimichurri sauce can be made 3 days in advance and kept in a nonreactive airtight container.

To grill the oysters, place them on a hot grill until they open, and serve with chimichurri sauce.

NOTE: For this dish, less esoteric oysters will do—Blue Point, Malpeque, or Texas Gulf. If an oyster does not open, do not eat it.

Mami's Gazpacho

Our at-home repertoire of dishes was often punctuated in the summer months with this standard.

3   ripe garden tomatoes, cut in half

2   roasted red bell peppers (fresh or jarred)

2   cloves garlic

1   green bell pepper

2   large cucumbers, peeled, seeded, and cut into chunks

1   large Spanish onion, cut into quarters

4¼ cups tomato juice

¼   cup olive oil

¼   cup sherry vinegar

½   teaspoon cumin

⅓   cup chopped fresh cilantro

⅓   cup chopped fresh flat-leaf parsley

Salt and pepper to taste

In a food processor fitted with the metal blade, place the tomatoes, red peppers, garlic, green pepper, cucumbers, and onion and puree. Using a rubber spatula, transfer the vegetable puree to a nonreactive bowl and add the tomato juice, olive oil, vinegar, and cumin. Allow the soup to sit for an hour at room temperature.

Strain the soup through a fine sieve and add the cilantro, parsley, salt, and pepper. Chill the gazpacho for several hours before serving.

NOTE: Chopped cucumber, onion, and bell pepper are a traditional garnish.

Grilled Mahimahi Steaks with Jalapeño-Mint-Compound Butter

1   cup (2 sticks) unsalted butter at room temperature

1   cup mint leaves, chopped

2   jalapeño peppers, minced

8   half-pound mahimahi steaks

In a small bowl, work the butter with a fork or use the paddle attachment of a standing mixer to combine the chopped mint and minced jalapeños. Using a rubber spatula, scoop the butter into a small bowl. The butter can be made 1 week in advance and kept covered in the refrigerator.

Grill the mahimahi on a hot grill for 4 minutes on each side, until flesh is opaque and flaky. Transfer the fish from the grill to a serving plate and place a spoonful of the compound butter on each piece of fish. Serve immediately.

NOTE: You can also cook in a grill pan on the stovetop, or sauté the fish in olive oil over medium-high heat, 3 minutes on each side until just browned. Reduce heat to low and cover for 3 minutes until light and flaky.

Corn on the Coals with Lime and Cayenne

2   dozen ears fresh corn in husk
Juice of 4 limes
1   teaspoon cayenne pepper

Microwave the corn for 3 minutes on high in 4 to 6 separate batches. Soak corn in room-temperature water for 3 minutes. Place the corn on the side of the coals or on a hot grill and grill for 10–15 minutes, turning constantly with tongs and allowing the husks to char. Pull back husks and remove silk before eating.

While the corn is grilling, combine the lime juice and cayenne pepper in a small bowl. Serve the corn hot with cayenne-lime juice.

NOTE: Can also be served with melted butter or grated queso blanco.

The white corn of Long Island should be a national treasure as far as we're all concerned. Corn is on almost all our summer menus. The cayenne adds a great kick.

Cuba Libre

In Little Havana, Miami, this drink is known as a "Mentirita," or a little lie, because Cuba is not yet free.

2 ounces white rum
Ice
8 ounces Coke
Lime wedge

Pour rum over ice and fill glass with Coke. Garnish with lime.

Salt-Rimmed Beer with Lime

Ice-cold cans of beer dipped in kosher salt, opened, and served with a wedge of lime in the opening.

Make this compote ahead
for an easy and delicious
beachside dessert.

Grilled Pineapple with Summer Berry Compote

1   cup superfine sugar

1   cup water

3   cups fresh blackberries, rinsed

2   cups fresh blueberries, rinsed and stems removed

2   cups sliced strawberries

2   ripe pineapples, peeled and cored

To make the berry compote, heat the sugar and water in a medium, heavy-bottomed saucepan over medium-high heat. Cook the mixture for 20–30 minutes until it reaches the consistency of syrup.

Add the blackberries, blueberries, and strawberries to the syrup and cook for an additional 15 minutes. Remove from heat and strain the berries into a bowl, returning the berry syrup to the saucepan. Continue to cook the syrup over medium heat until reduced by one quarter, about 15 minutes.

Pour the syrup over the berries and allow to cool. Berry compote can be made up to 3 days in advance and kept refrigerated in a nonreactive covered container.

To peel and core the pineapple, use a large, sharp knife to slice off the top and bottom. Place the pineapple standing up on one end, then cut from top to bottom all the way around to remove the skin.

To remove the core, cut the pineapple in half horizontally, giving you two whole rounds. Cut the pineapple halves in half lengthwise and again into quarters. Cut off the center core. Continue to cut these pieces in half again lengthwise. You should now have 16 spears of pineapple. Repeat the process with the second pineapple.

Pineapple can be cut a few hours in advance and kept in the refrigerator in an airtight nonreactive container.

To grill the pineapple, use a pair of tongs to transfer the spears to a hot grill and grill each side for 1–2 minutes, using the tongs to turn, until the pineapple starts to caramelize.

Serve the pineapple warm with berry compote.

Engagement Party Buffet

Three of us married late in our lives, and for a while it seemed we had a wedding every year, with friends and family gathering to toast the future. These nuptials all had a different spin for the cultures they introduced us to. Javier married Angela, a Colombian, teaching us the wonders of another Latin American country; Luli found Melchior, a German, and we found out that efficiency can coexist with *mañana;* and I met Amy, who taught us that Texas is indeed another country. One of the great things about weddings is the engagement parties that precede them. These parties give us the opportunity to meet the family of our sibling's future spouse.

MENU

White Gazpacho with Crab

Spanish Potato and Onion Tortilla

Avocado and Grapefruit Salad with Lime Vinaigrette

La Floridita Sandwiches

Picadillo Chile Rellenos

Sweet Rum Shrimp Skewers

Torticas de Moron

Mango Bellinis • Piña Coladas

WINE

Spanish Rosado

(Bodegas Nekeas Vega Sindoa)

Opposite: Torticas de Moron.　　　　　SERVES 12

If you've only had tomato-based gazpacho, this version will charm you with its bright flavors. The white color also works symbolically with a Catholic engagement.

White Gazpacho with Crab

4   cucumbers, peeled, seeded, and sliced

$\frac{1}{3}$ cup almonds

$\frac{1}{3}$ cup seedless green grapes

4   cloves garlic, sliced

3   stalks celery, washed and chopped

3   leeks, whites only, washed well

$3\frac{1}{2}$ cups vegetable stock

$\frac{1}{4}$ cup olive oil

2   tablespoons white wine vinegar

2   tablespoons fresh lemon juice

Salt and white pepper to taste

4   tablespoons mayonnaise (optional)

1   pound fresh crabmeat, picked over for cartilage

In a food processor fitted with the metal blade, puree the cucumber, almonds, grapes, garlic, celery, and leeks. Add half the vegetable stock and continue to puree. Using a spatula, transfer the vegetable puree to a large nonreactive bowl and stir in the remaining vegetable stock, olive oil, vinegar, lemon juice, salt, and pepper. Stir in the mayonnaise last, if wanted, to give it a creamy texture.

Serve the gazpacho in individual bowls and sprinkle with 2 tablespoons of the crabmeat.

NOTE: To keep the gazpacho white, use white ground pepper to season the soup. Gazpacho can be made one day in advance and kept in an airtight container.

Spanish Potato and Onion Tortilla

1   pound new potatoes, peeled

10 eggs

1/2 cup milk

2   teaspoons red pepper flakes (optional)

Salt and pepper to taste

1   medium Spanish onion, chopped

Preheat oven to 350 degrees. Grease a large braising pan or paella pan with lid.

Bring a large pot of water to a boil over high heat, add the potatoes, and boil until potatoes are just soft when pricked with a fork. Drain the potatoes and allow them to cool to room temperature. Slice them into rounds.

In a small bowl, whisk together the eggs, milk, red pepper flakes if wanted, salt, and pepper. Stir in the onion and sliced potatoes. Pour the egg mixture into the greased braising pan.

Cover and cook the tortilla over medium heat on the stovetop for 5 minutes, then transfer the pan to the oven and bake for 10–15 minutes until the egg mixture is set. Remove the cover and bake for an additional 10 minutes until the top is lightly browned.

Remove the pan from the oven and run a knife around the edge. Using a spatula, carefully work all the way around and underneath the tortilla to release it completely. Gently slip the tortilla onto a large serving plate.

If you only have a small pan to cook this dish in, divide the mixture and make two smaller ones.

This tortilla is much like a frittata. We served it so often at our parents' cocktail parties it was like another member of the family.

Avocado and Grapefruit Salad with Lime Vinaigrette

$\frac{2}{3}$ cup olive oil

Juice of 1 lime

Salt and pepper to taste

6 ripe Haas avocados, peeled, pitted, and sliced thick

4 pink grapefruit, peeled and sectioned

Combine olive oil, lime juice, salt, and pepper in a small jar with lid, cover tightly, and shake vigorously until the dressing is emulsified, about 30 seconds.

Arrange the avocado slices and grapefruit sections in an alternating pattern on a serving plate. Drizzle the vinaigrette over them and serve immediately.

NOTE: Avocados need to be perfectly ripe for this salad.

La Floridita was a favorite Hemingway haunt in Havana and the birthplace of the daiquiri. This little sandwich was the house specialty.

La Floridita Sandwiches

8 eggs

$\frac{1}{3}$ cup milk

20 thin slices white bread (Pepperidge Farm works best)

20 sandwich-sliced pickles

10 pieces thinly sliced ham

10 pieces thinly sliced Swiss cheese

5–6 tablespoons unsalted butter

3–4 teaspoons olive oil

In a large bowl, whisk together the eggs and milk. Set aside.

Use 2 slices of pickle and 1 slice each of ham and cheese per sandwich to make 10 sandwiches.

In a large skillet over medium heat, melt $\frac{1}{2}$ tablespoon butter and a teaspoon of olive oil. Dip the sandwiches one at a time into the egg mixture and fry until golden brown on both sides. Add more butter and oil as needed. Cut each sandwich into 4 triangles and serve.

Spanish Potato and Onion Tortilla and La Floridita Sandwiches.

This picadillo has great flavor, and at L-Ray making it a relleno turned an entrée into an appetizer and an easy-to-handle buffet dish.

Picadillo Chile Rellenos

2 pounds lean ground beef

4 tablespoons olive oil

2 large Spanish onions, finely chopped

10 cloves garlic, minced

4 roasted green peppers, diced

½ cup chopped Spanish green olives with pimento

½ cup raisins

⅓ cup capers

2 cups crushed tomatoes in juice

2 tablespoons dried oregano

Salt and pepper to taste

12 large poblano peppers, cored and seeded

Preheat oven to 350 degrees.

In a large skillet over medium-high heat, cook ground beef thoroughly and drain off fat. Add olive oil, onion, garlic, and green pepper and cook for 5 minutes until onion is soft. Add olives, raisins, capers, crushed tomatoes, oregano, salt, and pepper. Simmer over medium heat for 20 minutes. Remove from heat and allow to cool completely.

Stuff the poblano peppers with the picadillo filling. Arrange the peppers in a lightly greased roasting pan and bake for 35 minutes until the filling is heated through and the peppers are soft but not browned.

Picadillo can be made up to 3 days in advance and refrigerated in an airtight container. The peppers can be stuffed 1 day in advance and kept refrigerated in an airtight container.

Sweet Rum
Shrimp Skewers

1   cup freshly squeezed orange juice

1   cup dark rum

$\frac{1}{2}$ cup olive oil

$\frac{1}{4}$ cup sugar

Zest of 2 limes

2   cups cilantro leaves, chopped

3   dozen shrimp, peeled and deveined with tails on

In a medium mixing bowl, whisk together orange juice, dark rum, olive oil, and sugar. Stir in the lime zest and cilantro. Pour half the marinade in a nonreactive bowl. Add shrimp and pour remaining marinade over them. Cover with plastic wrap and marinate in the refrigerator for at least 1 hour and up to 3 hours.

Skewer shrimp and grill for 4 minutes, turning frequently so they cook evenly without burning.

NOTE: If using wooden skewers, soak overnight in water. Shrimp can also be cooked in a grill pan on the stovetop or under the broiler.

Mango Bellini

1   bottle champagne or sparkling wine

1   can mango nectar

Start with both ingredients chilled for a cold cocktail. Combine 2 parts champagne to 1 part nectar by the glass or the pitcher. In a pitcher, combine at the last minute to retain sparkle, and keep chilled in the refrigerator.

Piña Colada

4   ounces white rum

5   ounces pineapple juice, canned

2   ounces pineapple, canned or fresh

2   ounces Coco Lopez, canned

Crushed ice (helps to make a smooth drink)

Pineapple slices for garnish

Place all ingredients in blender and blend. Pour into a wineglass or highball glass and garnish with a slice of pineapple.

This cookie is from the small town of Moron in Cuba. It is our nanny Tati's signature cookie; she brings some to every reunion.

Torticas de Moron

6 cups flour

2½ cups confectioners' sugar

2 cups vegetable shortening

2 teaspoons lime zest

Preheat oven to 350 degrees.

In the bowl of a standing mixer fitted with the paddle attachment or in a large bowl with a wooden spoon, blend the flour, confectioners' sugar, shortening, and lime zest until it forms a smooth dough, about 3 minutes. Let the dough rest for 15 minutes wrapped in plastic.

To make the cookies, mold a small tablespoonful of dough into a football shape with your hands. Gently press the dough to flatten slightly and place on an ungreased cookie sheet.

Bake the cookies for 20–25 minutes. Cookies will be white and should not brown. Remove cookies and allow them to cool on a wire rack.

Just before serving, dust the cookies with confectioners' sugar and arrange on a serving plate.

MAKES ABOUT 40 COOKIES

Traditional Late Lunch in the Campo

With shadows starting to lengthen and friends staying for lunch, a rustic meal, Cuban style, is called for. These are all the standards from L-Ray's menu. With a little citrus in almost every dish and favorites like tostones and the guava empanadas, this is what we call comfort food.

MENU

SNAPPER CEVICHE

**BEET AND MANCHEGO SALAD
WITH CUMIN VINAIGRETTE**

GRILLED MARINATED PORK CHOPS WITH MOJO

TOSTONES

GUAVA AND CREAM CHEESE EMPANADAS

CAMPASINOS

WINE
PORTUGUESE VINHO VERDE
(CAVES DA CERCA FAMEGA)

CHILEAN MERLOT
(MONTES)

SERVES 6

Opposite: Snapper Ceviche.

At L-Ray I asked Jorge Adriazola to bring his Peruvian expertise with ceviche to this recipe. While in Peru there are a million variations, this is one you would probably find in Havana today.

Snapper Ceviche

3–4 red snapper fillets, scales and skin removed

1   cup (approximately 2–3 oranges) freshly squeezed orange juice

$\frac{1}{3}$ cup (approximately 1–2 limes) freshly squeezed lime juice

$\frac{1}{4}$ cup (approximately 1 lemon) freshly squeezed lemon juice

$\frac{1}{4}$ cup olive oil

$\frac{1}{2}$ red onion, finely chopped

1   jalapeño pepper. finely chopped

5   sprigs cilantro, finely chopped

Salt and pepper to taste

Zest of 2 oranges

Zest of 2 lemons

Zest of 2 limes

With a sharp knife, cut the fillets into $\frac{1}{2}$-inch chunks and place in a small nonreactive pan. In a small bowl, whisk together the orange juice, lime juice, lemon juice, and olive oil. Stir in red onion, jalapeño, cilantro, salt, and pepper and the zest of the orange, lemon, and lime. Pour the mixture over the fish to cover completely.

Cover the dish tightly with plastic wrap and place in the refrigerator for 3 hours, turning the fish once after the first hour and a half.

Remove the fish from the liquid and discard liquid. Serve chilled on small plates, in bowls, or in martini glasses.

NOTE: For this dish, have the fishmonger prepare 2 small snappers or other white fish, removing scales and skin, and cutting into 4 fillets.

Beet and Manchego Salad with Cumin Vinaigrette

3   large red beets, washed, stems and roots trimmed

1   large golden beet, washed, stems and roots trimmed

$\frac{1}{4}$ pound Manchego cheese

$\frac{1}{2}$ cup olive oil

$\frac{1}{3}$ cup white wine vinegar

3   cloves garlic, minced

1   tablespoon fresh lemon juice

1   teaspoon cumin

Salt and pepper to taste

Wrap the beets individually in aluminum foil and roast for $1\frac{1}{2}$–2 hours until tender when pricked with a fork. Allow the beets to cool long enough to handle them. Using a paring knife, remove the skins. Slice the beets, then cut into small cubes and set aside in a nonreactive bowl until cool.

Using a vegetable peeler, peel large, very thin slices of the Manchego cheese. Cover with plastic wrap and set aside.

In a glass jar with lid, combine the olive oil, vinegar, garlic, cumin, lemon juice, salt, and pepper. Close the lid tightly and shake vigorously until emulsified, about 30 seconds.

Arrange the golden beets on top of the red beets on a plate and drizzle with cumin dressing. Sprinkle the cheese over the beets and serve at room temperature for best flavor.

At Alva we had a favorite in a goat cheese and beet salad. Few people know that beets are a Cuban favorite, so at L-Ray we added cumin and Manchego to create a sister salad that was on the menu from day one.

Grilled Marinated Pork Chops with Mojo

10   cloves garlic

3   tablespoons dried oregano

$\frac{2}{3}$ cup olive oil

$\frac{1}{3}$ cup freshly squeezed orange juice

Juice of 2 limes

$\frac{1}{8}$ teaspoon cumin

Salt and pepper to taste

6   double-cut pork chops

Puree the garlic, oregano, olive oil, $\frac{1}{4}$ cup of the orange juice, lime juice, cumin, salt, and pepper in a blender or in a food processor fitted with the metal blade. Reserve $\frac{1}{3}$ cup of the mojo sauce and set aside.

To make the pork chop marinade, whisk the remaining $\frac{1}{2}$ cup of orange juice with the remaining mojo sauce in a nonreactive bowl. Place the pork chops in a nonreactive dish and add the marinade. Cover with plastic and marinate in the refrigerator for 1–2 hours, turning the pork occasionally.

Discard marinade and grill the pork chops on a hot grill for 5–7 minutes on each side until cooked to medium.

Serve with the reserved mojo sauce.

This dish is what Cubans are weaned on and live for. It might possibly have all the ingredients that make up Cuban cookery, with the exception of rum, of course.

Tío Armando roasting a pig, Cuban style, in South Carolina with Abuelo Manolo.

Opposite: Grilled Pork Chop, Beet Salad, and Tostones.

At the trendy birthplace of
Nuevo Latino, Yuca, they
topped this rustic standard
with crème fraiche and caviar.
Not bad, but we love mojo
and can't get enough of it.
If you're short on time, a
squeeze of lime and some
sea salt taste great.

Tostones

4   cups vegetable oil

3–4 green plantains, peeled and cut into 1½-inch slices

Salt to taste

In a deep pot, heat the vegetable oil until hot, about 350 degrees. Fry
the plantain slices in 4 batches until golden in color. Remove the
fried plantains with a slotted spoon or tongs to a paper towel.

When the fried plantains are cool enough to handle, flatten them
with the heel of your hand, a rolling pin, or a canned product.
Reheat the oil and fry the flattened plantain again until golden
brown and warmed through. Drain on paper towel, sprinkle with
salt, and serve immediately.

Campasino

2   ounces white rum

2   ounces Coco Lopez

1   ounce Cointreau

1   ounce lime juice

Fresh mint for garnish

Combine ingredients in a shaker and shake.
Pour over fresh ice and garnish with mint.

Guava and Cream Cheese Empanadas

3   cups all-purpose flour

½   pound (2 sticks) unsalted butter, chilled

1½ teaspoon salt

½   cup cold water

1   egg

1   tablespoon water

Guava paste

Cream cheese

Preheat oven to 400 degrees. Lightly grease baking sheet.

In a food processor fitted with the metal blade, mix the flour, butter, and salt. Pulse until the mixture resembles rough cornmeal. While motor is running, slowly add the water through the feed tube until dough just starts to form a ball.

Remove dough from bowl and form a ball. Wrap in plastic and allow to rest for 30 minutes.

In a small bowl, make an egg wash by whisking the egg and water together, and set aside. Roll the dough out on a floured surface to a ⅛-inch thickness. Using a 4-inch round cutter, cut out dough.

Place 1 teaspoon of guava paste with 1 teaspoon of cream cheese in the center of each round. Using a pastry brush, brush the egg wash completely around the inside edge of the dough. Fold dough over to form a crescent, and pinch edges between thumb and forefinger to create a fluted edging and seal the filling.

Place the empanadas on a lightly greased baking sheet and coat each one with egg wash. Bake for 20–25 minutes or until golden brown. Allow to cool slightly before serving.

MAKES 2 DOZEN

Along with natilla, this pastry was as much a part of our childhood as running out of hot water if you were the last to take a bath.

Javier and Angela's Bridgehampton home.

Early Fall Gathering

Although paella can be a one-pot meal, no one seems to complain when my brother Ale and his friend Kendall, the best cooks in the family, add a couple of extra dishes. When the word gets out that they are cooking, our cars start to show up at their home, as if a dinner bell rang.

MENU

PAPI'S MARINATED OLIVES

ROPA VIEJA EMPANADAS

ROASTED RED PEPPER SOUP

MAMI'S PAELLA

JICAMA, ORANGE, AVOCADO, AND RADISH SALAD
WITH LIME DRESSING

DARK RUM BANANAS FOSTER

MOJITOS

WINE
MANZANILLA
(HIDALGO LA GITANA)

PORTUGUESE PERIQUITA
(QUINTA DE PARROTES)

SERVES 4 TO 6

Opposite: Mami's Paella.

My father has been making these olives for years and we teased him every time until one day, one of us tried them. They couldn't be easier or tastier.

Papi's Marinated Olives

10-ounce jar Spanish olives with pimiento

3 tablespoons Worcestershire sauce

1 teaspoon Tabasco sauce

In a small bowl, combine olives, Worcestershire sauce, and Tabasco; toss to coat evenly. Cover bowl with plastic and refrigerate for at least 30 minutes, mixing occasionally. The longer the olives marinate, the stronger and better the taste.

Ropa vieja literally translates to "old clothes" but refers to the shredded meat in this classic Cuban country dish. We hated this dish as kids . . . how times have changed.

Ropa Vieja Empanadas

FILLING

$\frac{1}{4}$ cup olive oil

6 cloves garlic, minced

2 medium Spanish onions, chopped

2 roasted green bell peppers, chopped

$\frac{1}{2}$ cup dry white wine

12-ounce can diced tomatoes in juice

$1\frac{1}{2}$ teaspoons dried oregano

1 bay leaf

Salt and pepper to taste

$1\frac{1}{4}$ pound flank steak

DOUGH

3 cups all-purpose flour

2 sticks unsalted butter, cubed

$1\frac{1}{2}$ teaspoons salt

$\frac{1}{2}$ cup plus 1 tablespoon very cold water

1 egg

In a large braising pan with lid, heat olive oil over medium-high heat and sauté the sofrito of garlic, onion, and roasted pepper until soft. Add the white wine to deglaze the pan and stir. Stir in the tomato, oregano, bay leaf, salt, and pepper. Add the flank steak and cover.

Reduce heat to medium and cook the flank steak for 35 minutes or until it is cooked through. Remove flank steak from pan and reduce heat to low. Allow the flank steak to cool enough to handle while the sauce reduces until thick. Remove from heat. Using your fingers and a fork, pull or shred the steak and add back to sauce. Allow the mixture to cool to room temperature.

While the filling is cooking, make the dough. In a food processor fitted with the metal blade, combine the flour, butter, and salt. Pulse until the mixture resembles rough cornmeal. While the motor is running, pour the $\frac{1}{2}$ cup cold water through the feed tube until dough just forms a ball. Remove dough from bowl, form a ball, and press lightly to flatten. Wrap dough in plastic and refrigerate for at least 30 minutes.

Preheat oven to 400 degrees.

In a small bowl, whisk together the egg and 1 tablespoon water to make an egg wash. Roll dough out on a floured surface to a $\frac{1}{8}$-inch thickness. Use a 4-inch round cutter to cut out rounds. Using a small pastry brush, brush the egg wash completely around the inside edge of the dough and place a tablespoon of drained filling in the center. Fold the dough over to form a crescent and press edges together to seal. Use the back of a fork to seal the edges and create a rustic edging.

Brush each empanada with egg wash and place on a lightly greased baking sheet. Bake for 30 minutes or until golden brown. Serve hot.

MAKES 2 DOZEN

Fernando and Isabel enjoy a brisk ride.

Roasted Red Pepper Soup

¼ cup olive oil

2 medium Spanish onions, quartered

2 cloves garlic

5 roasted red bell peppers

1 cup tomato juice

4 cups chicken stock or vegetable stock

1 teaspoon dried oregano

½ teaspoon cumin

Salt and pepper to taste

In a medium stockpot, heat the olive oil until hot but not smoking and sauté the onion and garlic until soft. Add the red pepper and continue sautéing until the peppers begin to fall apart. Add the tomato juice, stock, oregano, cumin, salt, and pepper and allow to come just to a boil, then remove from heat.

Puree the soup in a food processor fitted with a metal blade or blender until smooth and return to pot to reheat. Serve the soup hot.

Paella always meant a special occasion with special friends. Our mother would be excited to prepare it and beamed with pride as she delivered it to the table for guests and family.

Mami's Paella

⅓ cup olive oil

5 chicken drumsticks

4 small chorizo sausages, diced

4 plum tomatoes, seeded and diced

4 cloves garlic, minced

1 large Spanish onion, diced

½ pound small raw shrimp

¾ pound mussels, cleaned

2 cups arborio rice

2½ cups chicken stock

½ cup tomato sauce

1 cup frozen peas

6–8 saffron threads

1 roasted green bell pepper, chopped

In a large heavy paella pan, braising pan, or Dutch oven with lid, heat the olive oil over medium-high heat and brown chicken on all sides. Remove chicken from pan and add the chorizo, tomatoes, garlic, and onion, sautéing for 5 minutes. Add the shrimp and mussels, cover dish, and reduce heat to medium, cooking for 5 minutes. Remove the shrimp and mussels to a separate bowl.

Add rice and stir for 1 minute. Add chicken stock, tomato sauce, peas, saffron, and chicken legs. Cover dish and reduce heat to medium-low, cooking for 20 minutes until the rice is tender. Add the roasted green pepper and bake in oven for 15 minutes.

Remove paella from the oven and add the shrimp and mussels, mix well, and bake for an additional 5 minutes until heated through. Serve immediately.

NOTE: Do not eat any mussels that do not open from the heat of cooking.

Jicama, Orange, Avocado, and Radish Salad with Lime Dressing

²⁄₃ cup olive oil

Juice of 1 lime

Salt and pepper to taste

½ medium jicama, grated

2 oranges, peeled and sectioned

2 avocados, peeled, pitted, and sliced

4 radishes, washed and thinly sliced

To make the dressing: Place the olive oil, lime juice, salt, and pepper in a small jar. Close the lid tightly and shake vigorously for 30 seconds to emulsify. Taste to adjust seasoning and set aside.

Prepare salad ingredients. If preparing the salad in advance, keep the jicama, orange sections, and radish slices individually wrapped in the refrigerator until ready to serve. Reserve the avocado for slicing just before serving. Do not prepare the salad ingredients more than 2 hours prior to serving, as the ingredients will dry out.

To serve: Evenly divide the jicama between salad plates and arrange orange sections, avocado slices, and radish slices on top. Drizzle dressing over each salad and serve.

Jicama couldn't be more foreboding, but like many an old Cuban, if you can get past the cantankerous outer layer there lies a heart of gold. The flesh has a wonderful pear and celery flavor.

Rum was actually a product of the American colonies, but we Cubans like to call it our own. Add bananas to the formula and it's hard to believe that we didn't invent this dessert first.

Dark Rum Bananas Foster

⅓ cup dark brown sugar

1⅓ cup (¾ stick) unsalted butter

½ cup heavy cream

1 teaspoon vanilla

2 tablespoons dark rum

4–6 ripe bananas, peeled and sliced lengthwise

In a heavy, medium saucepan, melt the brown sugar and butter together over medium heat. When sugar is completely dissolved, stir in the heavy cream and vanilla until well blended. Remove from heat and stir in the rum.

In a large skillet, preferably nonstick, heat ⅓ cup of the caramel rum sauce and cook the bananas over medium heat, until warmed through and soft, about 2 minutes per side.

Serve hot with the warm caramel rum sauce.

Mojito

4–5 fresh mint leaves

1 ounce simple syrup

1 ounce lime juice

2 ounces white rum

Ice

Club soda

Mint

Lime wedge

Muddle well mint, simple syrup, and lime juice in the bottom of a glass. Fill glass with ice, add rum, and top with soda. Quickly pour ingredients from one glass into another and back. Garnish with mint and lime wedge.

Stormy, Surfing, and Refueling

Whether in the Hamptons, Malibu, or Mundaka, Spain, if there is an ocean nearby we are thinking, "How long until we go surfing?" Rain or shine, the first to arrive at the beach will get a call: what does the water look like? If there is a "bump," we are there riding waves, with or without boards. When we get out of the water we are worn out, but the taste of saltwater on our lips and the cold water invigorates us. We run, bike, or ride home to refuel with an easy meal full of seasonal flavor.

MENU

CORN CHOWDER WITH ROASTED GREEN CHILIES

LATIN CAPRESE SALAD

**GRILLED FISH SANDWICH WITH CHIPOTLE MAYONNAISE
OR PINEAPPLE RELISH**

TEQUILA OR RUM SUNRISES

COLD BEER

SERVES 4

*Opposite: Corn Chowder with Roasted Green Chilies, Grilled Fish
Sandwich with Chipotle Mayonnaise, and Latin Caprese Salad.*

Corn Chowder with Roasted Green Chilies

5 tablespoons unsalted butter

¼ cup white onion, minced

1 clove garlic, minced

4 cups corn kernels, fresh or frozen

4 cups chicken stock

⅔ cup heavy cream

Salt and pepper to taste

3 roasted jalapeño peppers, chopped

In a heavy saucepan over medium-high heat, melt the butter and sauté the onion until translucent. Add garlic and corn kernels, tossing in the butter to coat for 1 minute, being careful not to brown the corn kernels. Add the chicken stock and reduce heat to low. Cook for 15 minutes stirring occasionally.

In the jar of a blender, puree the corn mixture in batches. (Cover blender to prevent hot liquid splatter.) Pour the pureed corn mixture through a fine sieve, pressing to remove the corn-kernel skin. Return the soup to the saucepan and add cream, salt, and pepper. Heat until just hot, taste and adjust seasoning.

Serve the soup with a sprinkle of chopped roasted jalapeño peppers.

The brothers take to the surf.

Latin Caprese Salad

$^1/_3$ cup olive oil

2   tablespoons fresh lime juice

Salt and pepper to taste

3   ripe garden tomatoes, sliced

$^1/_3$ pound queso fresco cheese, crumbled

$^1/_4$ cup fresh cilantro leaves, chopped

$^1/_4$ cup fresh basil, chopped

This is a Latin take on the Italian classic. We think it's tastier than the original that inspired it.

To make the vinaigrette, combine olive oil, lime juice, salt, and pepper in a small jar with lid, cover tightly, and shake vigorously until the vinaigrette is emulsified, about 30 seconds. Taste to adjust seasoning and set aside.

On a serving platter, arrange the tomatoes in a circular pattern. Sprinkle the crumbled cheese and herbs over the tomatoes. Drizzle the lime vinaigrette over the salad, and season with salt and pepper.

NOTE: Best if tomatoes are in season and the tomatoes and cheese are kept and served at room temperature.

Javier and Fernando.

Tequila or Rum Sunrise

2   ounces tequila or rum

Ice

4   ounces orange juice

Grenadine

Pour tequila or rum over ice and add juice. Add several splashes of grenadine as a float; it will sink, creating the "sunrise."

Grilled Fish Sandwich with Chipotle Mayonnaise or Pineapple Relish

$^1\!/_4$ cup olive oil

Juice of $^1\!/_2$ a lime

Salt and pepper to taste

4   7-ounce Chilean sea bass fillets, bones removed (grouper, cod, red snapper, halibut, or mahimahi can all be substituted)

MAYONNAISE

1   egg

1   egg yolk

Juice of 1 lime

$^1\!/_2$ chipotle pepper (canned in sauce), or to taste

1   teaspoon salt

$^1\!/_2$ teaspoon black pepper

1   cup olive oil

4   potato hamburger buns, toasted

In a small nonreactive bowl, whisk together the ¼ cup olive oil, juice of ½ a lime, and salt and pepper to taste. Pour the marinade into a nonreactive dish and add the fish, turning over once or twice to completely coat. Allow to marinate for 10 minutes, turning once.

While the fish is marinating, make the mayonnaise. In the jar of a blender, place the egg, egg yolk, lime juice, chipotle pepper, salt, and pepper and blend for 30 seconds on high. While the motor is running, gradually pour the olive oil through the top in a continuous, thin stream until the mayonnaise is thick and creamy.

On a hot grill, grill the fish approximately 6 minutes on each side, until the flesh is opaque and flaky.

Serve the fish on toasted potato buns with chipotle mayonnaise or Pineapple Relish (recipe follows).

NOTE: You can also cook in a grill pan on the stovetop, or sauté the fish in olive oil over medium-high heat, 3 minutes on each side until just browned. Reduce heat to low and cover for 3 minutes until light and flaky.

Pineapple Relish

2   1-inch-thick slices fresh pineapple

2   half-inch slices red onion

½   jalapeño

½   teaspoon virgin olive oil

Juice of 1 lime

1   teaspoon chopped mint

1   teaspoon chopped cilantro

Salt and pepper to taste

Heat grill or grill pan until hot.

Grill the pineapple, onion, and jalapeño just until slightly colored. Remove from grill and allow to cool to room temperature, then dice.

In a nonreactive bowl, combine the grilled pineapple mixture with the olive oil, lime juice, mint, cilantro, salt, and pepper and mix until combined.

Serve at room temperature.

MAKES ROUGHLY ½ CUP

Cuban Thanksgiving

Thanksgiving is the fall's big gathering. The kitchen is always crowded, with Ale passing Luli the daiquiri under Kendall's arm, while he is putting the bird in the oven. I'm balancing a glass of wine and reaching for a boniato handoff from Angela. The table is a long one on this day. We manage to blend some of our favorite Cuban flavors with this quintessential American holiday. We have a lot to be thankful for.

Above: A toast of thanks for the blessing of family.
Opposite: Cumin-and-Oregano-Rubbed Turkey
with Chorizo-and-Cornbread Stuffing.

SQUASH SOUP WITH PUMPKIN SEED OIL

MASHED BONIATO AND ORANGE IN ORANGE SHELL

STEAMED YUCA WITH MOJO

AVOCADO, ORANGE AND PINEAPPLE SALAD
WITH TROPICAL BASIL VINAIGRETTE

CONGRIS

WILTED COLLARDS AND TOMATO WITH BACON

CUMIN-AND-OREGANO-RUBBED TURKEY
WITH CHORIZO-AND-CORNBREAD STUFFING

MANGO CRANBERRY SAUCE

CUBAN COFFEE

PUMPKIN FLAN

CLASSIC DAIQUIRIS

CAPARINAS

WINE
SPANISH ALBARINO
(PAZO DE SENORANS)

ARGENTINE SYRAH
(GRAFFIGNA)

SERVES 10 TO 12

Tati serving Congris (black beans and rice).

Squash Soup
with Pumpkin Seed Oil

2   large acorn squash

1   medium sugar pumpkin

1   large sweet dumpling squash or acorn

4   tablespoons olive oil

1   medium Spanish onion, chopped

4   cloves garlic

1   roasted green bell pepper

4   cups chicken stock

1   bay leaf

½   teaspoon cumin

Salt and pepper to taste

Pumpkin seed oil (optional)

Preheat oven to 400 degrees.

   To prepare the squash and pumpkin, quarter and seed them. Place them on a roasting pan and drizzle with olive oil, using your fingers to coat the entire surface.

   Roast the squash and pumpkin until soft, about 40 minutes, and remove from the oven. Allow to cool long enough to handle, then use a paring knife to remove the skin and cut the squash and pumpkin into smaller chunks. Set aside.

   In a large heavy stockpot, heat the olive oil over medium-high heat. Make sofrito by chopping onion, garlic, and roasted green pepper, sautéing until soft and falling apart. Add chicken stock, bay leaf, and cumin, stirring for 1 minute. Add the squash and pumpkin and allow the soup to simmer over medium heat for 45–60 minutes until it is reduced by one quarter and the squash is completely soft.

   Remove the bay leaf. Using a regular blender, puree the soup. (Cover blender with a towel to prevent hot liquid spatter.) Taste the soup and adjust the seasoning with salt and pepper. Serve hot with a drizzle of pumpkin seed oil, if desired.

A friend and great wine importer in New York, Michael Skurnik, imports a German pumpkin seed oil that is equal to truffle oil in its fragrance and makes this soup outrageous. We first made this soup for my wedding rehearsal dinner at Alva and it was on the menu the next week.

Tati and Alejandro in the kitchen.

Mashed Boniato and Orange in Orange Shell

3 pounds boniato, washed

¾ cup (1½ sticks) unsalted butter

Salt and pepper to taste

8–10 oranges

Preheat the oven to 350 degrees.

Roast the boniato on a baking sheet for 45 minutes or until soft when pricked with a fork. Allow to cool long enough to handle. Using a paring knife, peel the skin off and place in a large bowl.

While the boniato is roasting, prepare the orange shells. Using a sharp knife, slice the top ⅓ of the orange off. Take a small slice off the bottom of the orange, just enough to make the orange stand up without rolling, being careful not to cut into the fruit.

Use a paring or grapefruit knife to hollow out the bottom half of the orange in a cone shape to create a serving dish for the mashed boniato. Squeeze the juice from the removed part of the oranges and reserve in a nonreactive bowl.

When the boniato is ready, use a potato masher to mash it with the butter and reserved orange juice. Add salt and pepper.

Spoon or pipe the mashed boniato (with a large pastry bag fitted with a large round tip) into the orange shells. Put the filled oranges on a baking sheet and place under the broiler until the boniato turns just golden in color. Serve immediately.

NOTE: For an elegant appearance, wrap the orange in parchment strips to shape and support the boniato mash over the edge of the orange. Remove to serve.

Javier.

Steamed Yuca with Mojo

3   pounds frozen yuca

10 cloves garlic

4   cups oregano leaves

Juice of 2 limes

¾   cup olive oil

¼   cup freshly squeezed orange juice

⅛   teaspoon cumin

Salt and pepper to taste

Steam the yuca in the basket of a vegetable steamer over medium-high heat for 30 minutes.

While the yuca is steaming, puree the garlic, oregano, lime juice, olive oil, orange juice, cumin, salt, and pepper in the jar of a blender or in a food processor fitted with a metal blade. Taste and adjust seasoning. Serve yuca hot with mojo sauce.

Thanksgiving preparations and conversation.

Avocado, Orange, and Pineapple Salad with Tropical Basil Vinaigrette

20-ounce can crushed pineapple, drained, juice reserved

1   cup olive oil

¾   cup white wine vinegar

2   cloves garlic, minced

4   tablespoons chopped basil

Salt and pepper to taste

3   avocados, peeled, pitted, and sliced

3   oranges, peeled and sectioned

In a small container with lid, place the pineapple juice, olive oil, vinegar, garlic, basil, salt, and pepper. Close the lid tightly and shake vigorously; set aside.

Arrange avocado slices and orange sections on a plate, spoon crushed pineapple over them, and drizzle with tropical basil vinaigrette. Serve immediately.

Congris

3   cups black bean soup, homemade (page 138) or canned, hot

3   cups cooked white rice, hot

Salt and pepper to taste

In a large bowl, combine the black bean soup with the rice, toss, and season with salt and pepper to taste. Serve hot.

NOTE: The black beans can be freshly made or doctored from canned beans for this dish.

Also known as *Morros y Cristianos*, this translates to Moors and Christians, referring to the black beans and white rice, a leftover from the Arabic incursion into Spain. The thought of the two living in peace seems appropriate for Thanksgiving.

This vegetable dish reflects the Southern influence of our maternal grandmother Gui Gui's home in South Carolina.

Wilted Collards and Tomato with Bacon

2 bunches collard greens, washed and with stems removed

6 slices thick-cut bacon, cooked

3 tablespoons olive oil

4 cloves garlic, sliced

4 ripe plum tomatoes, seeded and chopped

Salt and pepper to taste

Using a sharp knife, cut the collard greens into shreds. In a large skillet, cook the bacon until crisp and drain on a paper towel. Reserve 2 tablespoons of bacon fat. Crumble the bacon and set aside.

Add 2 tablespoons olive oil to the bacon fat and heat until hot. Add the garlic and cook for one minute. Add half the shredded collard greens and sauté until wilted. Add the tomatoes and crumbled bacon, stir, and add the remaining collard greens. If necessary cook the collards with tomato and bacon in two batches.

Season with salt and pepper and serve hot.

Lisa helping Jackie.

Cumin-and-Oregano-Rubbed Turkey with Chorizo-and-Cornbread Stuffing

16-pound turkey, fresh or defrosted

3–4 cups Cornbread Stuffing (recipe follows)

Kitchen string

Cumin Rub (recipe follows)

1½ cups (3 sticks) unsalted butter

The truth is that our Thanksgiving turkey is an annual experiment because the turkey preparation job is taken on by a different sibling every year. This recipe is one of my favorites.

Preheat the oven to 400 degrees.

Remove the plastic piece from the legs of the turkey, if necessary, and the gizzard package and neck from the cavity. Rinse the turkey inside and out with very cold water and pat dry with paper towels.

Loosely stuff the turkey with the stuffing. Pull the legs together so that they overlap. Use the kitchen string to tie the legs together. Spoon any leftover cornbread stuffing into a buttered ovenproof casserole dish. Bake in a 350-degree oven, uncovered, for 20–25 minutes, or until crispy and golden brown.

Using your hands, gently rub about half to three quarters of the cumin rub over the exterior of the turkey, working it lightly into the skin. Reserve the remaining rub for basting the turkey during roasting.

Place the turkey on a rack in a large roasting pan. Roast uncovered for 30 minutes until the skin starts to brown, then cover with aluminum foil.

Meanwhile, in a small saucepan, melt the 3 sticks of butter over medium heat. Stir in the remaining rub. Set aside, covered, to keep warm. Use a pastry brush to baste the turkey with the seasoned butter every 30 minutes during roasting.

Reduce the heat to 325 degrees and roast the turkey for about 4½ hours, or until the juices run clear when the meat is pricked, the leg joints feel loose, and a meat thermometer registers 180 degrees when inserted in the thickest part of the thigh. Check the stuffing: the thermometer should register 165 degrees when inserted into the center of the stuffing.

Classic Daiquiri

2 ounces white rum

1 ounce simple syrup

1 ounce lime juice

Ice

Combine all ingredients in a shaker, shake, and strain into a chilled martini glass.

CUMIN RUB

$\frac{1}{2}$ cup (1 stick) unsalted butter

2 tablespoons cumin

5 tablespoons dried oregano

3 tablespoons smoked paprika (hot)

2 tablespoons salt

2 tablespoons fresh-cracked pepper

$\frac{1}{4}$ cup olive oil

In a small saucepan, melt the butter over medium heat.

Combine the seasonings and olive oil in a mixing bowl. Add the melted butter and stir to mix well. Set aside to cool to room temperature.

CORNBREAD STUFFING

4 $8\frac{1}{2}$-ounce boxes cornbread mix

1 cup toasted pine nuts

1 cup (2 sticks) unsalted butter, melted

2 large Spanish onions, chopped

10 cloves garlic, minced

4 small (7 ounces) chorizo sausages, diced

2 roasted red bell peppers, chopped

1 cup fresh oregano, chopped

Salt and pepper to taste

Bake the cornbread according to package directions. While the bread is still warm, cut it into small cubes in the pan. Let the bread sit at room temperature, uncovered, for 12 hours or overnight. Remove the bread from the pan and crumble to make coarse breadcrumbs.

To toast the pine nuts, bake them on a baking sheet in a 300-degree oven for approximately 5 minutes until they turn golden brown. Watch carefully as they will burn fast. Immediately remove the nuts from the pan to a clean dish to stop them cooking.

In a medium sauté pan, melt the butter over medium heat. Sauté the onion and garlic until translucent but not browned, about 5 minutes.

In a large bowl, combine the breadcrumbs, pine nuts, sautéed onion and garlic, sausages, red pepper and oregano, mixing well. Season to taste with salt and pepper. The stuffing can be made up to this point a day in advance and kept refrigerated in an airtight container.

Reserve 3 to 4 cups of the stuffing to stuff the turkey.

Mango Cranberry Sauce

12-ounce bag fresh cranberries
¾ cup mango nectar
½ cup sugar

In a heavy saucepan, heat the cranberries, mango nectar, and sugar over medium heat. Cook the cranberries for 15–20 minutes until they begin to pop and the sauce thickens. Remove the cranberry sauce from heat and allow to cool to room temperature before serving.

Cranberry sauce can be made up to 1 week in advance and kept refrigerated in an airtight container.

MAKES 2 CUPS

When we first tried this combination, there were skeptics, but now it's been on the Thanksgiving table for years and is a perfect metaphor for the term "Cuban American."

Cuban Coffee

6 cups water
6 tablespoons espresso coffee, finely ground
6 tablespoons sugar

Make the coffee any way you prefer. Pour one hot cup coffee into sugar and mix until it becomes a paste. Serve in demitasse cups, adding equal amounts of this paste and remaining coffee.

This rocket fuel could jump-start the Cuban space program.

Capariña

1   lime, sliced into quarters

1   ounce simple syrup

Crushed ice

2   ounces Cachaca

Place lime quarters and simple syrup in glass and muddle to squeeze all juice from limes. Transfer to a shaker, add crushed ice and Cachaca, and shake.

Pour into highball glass and serve. The muddle of this cocktail brings out the oil and meat of the limes, so we don't want to strain this drink.

Pumpkin Flan

1^3/$_4$ cup sugar

1^1/$_2$ cups whole milk

^{1}/$_2$ cup unflavored canned pumpkin puree

1   cinnamon stick

^{1}/$_4$ teaspoon salt

3   eggs

3   egg yolks

1   tablespoon pure vanilla extract

Preheat oven to 350 degrees.

In a heavy saucepan melt 1 cup sugar over medium-high heat, stirring occasionally, until the sugar is amber in color and has turned into a smooth liquid. Immediately remove the syrup from heat and pour evenly into the bottom of a heated 9-inch glass pie plate, 2-quart casserole dish, or a cake mold. (To heat the dish, pour hot or boiling water into it and let stand for a minute or two, then drain and dry completely before adding the sugar syrup.)

In a heavy saucepan, bring the milk, pumpkin puree, cinnamon stick, and salt to a boil over medium heat and remove from heat immediately. Discard the cinnamon stick.

In a large mixing bowl beat together the eggs, egg yolks, remaining sugar, and vanilla. While the beater is running, slowly add ^{1}/$_2$ cup of the hot milk mixture and beat until eggs are tempered, then slowly add the remaining hot milk.

Pour the mixture into the dish over the hardened sugar syrup and place in a baking pan. Add hot water to halfway up the side of the dish. Place in oven and cook for 1 hour or until the custard has set.

Carefully remove the baking pan from the oven and remove the flan dish from the hot water bath and allow to cool. While the flan is still warm, run a knife around the edge to loosen it.

To remove flan, place a large, deep plate face down on top of the dish and invert the flan onto the plate. Make sure the plate is large enough to hold the flan and has enough of a well to hold the syrup.

Flan can be served warm or chilled. The flan can be prepared 2 days in advance and kept covered and refrigerated.

Monday Night Football Party

Jorge and Javier's favorite team is the Green Bay Packers. If they're playing on Monday night, we're together cheering for the team from the frozen tundra while we eat some easy-to-make family favorites like Cuban sandwiches. At our first restaurant, Alva, we served American bistro food and had a great bar with authentic Cuban cigar smoke. We miss Miami's great Cuban sandwich shops, so we started making Cuban sandwiches for lunch at the bar. We explained them to a local. He said, "That sounds like a Cuban Rueben." We changed the spelling and trademarked it!

MENU

SPICY PEPITAS

JORGE'S CHILI

CUBAN RUBAN PRESSED SANDWICHES

MANGO SORBET WITH GRAND MARNIER

TOP-SHELF TEQUILA WITH SANGRITA SIDES

ICED NEGRO MODELOS AND LIME

SERVES 6 TO 8

Opposite: Jorge's Chili.

Served at the L-Ray bar
on opening day. These
seeds are addictive.

Spicy Pepitas

3 small sugar pumpkins, seeded

2 teaspoons kosher salt

1$\frac{1}{2}$ teaspoons cracked black pepper

$\frac{1}{2}$ teaspoon cayenne pepper

Preheat oven to 350 degrees.

Wash seeds and lightly dry them with a paper towel. Spread them evenly over a heavy baking sheet. In a small bowl combine the salt, pepper, and cayenne pepper and sprinkle evenly over the seeds. Bake for 10–12 minutes until golden brown.

Serve warm or at room temperature.

Javier and Fernando enjoy a late-fall sunset.

Jorge's Chili

5   roasted green bell peppers, diced

2   1-pound cans pinto beans

2   1-pound cans black beans

2   1-pound cans great northern white beans

2   1-pound cans kidney beans

$\frac{1}{3}$ cup olive oil

2   medium Spanish onions, diced

2   jalapeño peppers, diced

8   cloves garlic, minced

6   cups (two 28-ounce cans) chopped tomatoes in juice

1   can tomato paste

2   teaspoons cayenne pepper

2   teaspoons ground cumin

Salt and pepper to taste

Sour cream

Grated Monterey Jack cheese

Crushed tortilla chips

Jorge, the eldest brother, is our family's writer. He's a movie producer with a yen for chili. His cannot be beat. We started eating this chili in the 1970s and have not found a better one since.

Slice the tops off the peppers and remove seeds and membrane. Slice the peppers in half and place them on a baking sheet cut side down. Broil for 10 minutes until black and charred. Use a paring knife to remove skin when cool enough to handle.

While peppers are roasting, thoroughly rinse the beans under cold water in a large colander and set aside.

In a large, heavy stockpot, sauté the onions and jalapeños in olive oil over medium-high heat for 3 minutes; add garlic and sauté 2 minutes more.

Stir in chopped tomatoes and tomato paste. Add beans, roasted peppers, cayenne pepper, and cumin and stir to combine. Bring the chili just to a boil and reduce heat to medium-low, allowing it to simmer for 30 minutes. Taste and adjust seasoning with salt and pepper.

Serve with sour cream, grated Monterey Jack cheese, and crushed tortilla chips.

Cuban Ruban
Pressed Sandwiches

2   1-pound pork tenderloins

Salt and pepper to taste

6   Cuban sweet rolls or 1 loaf challah bread

Yellow mustard

1   jar sandwich-cut dill pickles

$\frac{1}{4}$ pound thinly sliced ham

$\frac{1}{4}$ pound thinly sliced Swiss cheese

Preheat oven to 350 degrees.

Salt and pepper the pork loins. In a large, heavy, ovenproof skillet over high heat, brown the pork loins and transfer the skillet to the oven. Roast pork loins for 25 minutes or until cooked through or an instant-read thermometer reads 160 degrees. Allow the pork to rest for 10 minutes before slicing thinly.

Slice Cuban roll lengthwise or challah bread in $\frac{1}{2}$-inch-thick slices, smear mustard on six pieces of the bread, and layer 2 or 3 pickle slices on top of the mustard, then 3 slices of pork, 1 slice of ham, and 1 slice of Swiss cheese. Place these open-faced on a baking sheet and broil for 2 minutes or until cheese is melted. Remove from oven and add top slice of bread.

The sandwiches are meant to be pressed flat while cooking. If you own a sandwich press or a waffle iron with interchangeable flat grids, heat it to high and press the sandwiches until brown on both sides and cheese is melted.

Other options are as follows: in a large, lightly greased skillet, brown the sandwich while pressing with either a cast-iron pan, a dinner plate with a large can of soup or beans on top of it, or an aluminum-foil-wrapped brick. Cook for 2 minutes on each side.

Cut sandwiches in quarters and serve hot.

Mango Sorbet
with Grand Marnier

Mango sorbet (1 cup per person)

Grand Marnier

Serve your favorite brand of mango sorbet in individual bowls, drizzled with Grand Marnier.

Not everyone wants dessert after beer and tequila, but if the Packers win, we somehow find the room to celebrate!

Top-Shelf Tequila with Sangrita Side

Reposado and añejo tequilas are both made to be sipped, not unlike single-malt scotches. Traditionally, Mexicans sip these spirits with a chaser called sangrita, not to be confused with sangria. There are many versions of sangrita citrus-based chasers.

Pick your favorite reposado or añejo tequila and serve neat in a highball glass.

Sangrita

2   ounces orange juice

1   ounce tomato juice

$1/2$ ounce lime juice

4   splashes of Tabasco sauce

Combine all ingredients in a shaker, shake, serve neat along with aged tequila.

Christmas Eve Mariscada

One of our favorite Christmas Eve dinners came from a story my mother told us about a wonderful dinner she had. It was a Christmas in Spain where all the dishes were seafood (*mariscada* means of the sea). Whole fish are at once rustic, celebratory, and beautiful. Black beans are a tradition at every Cuban Christmas Eve table, and the shrimp tamales are wrapped in banana leaf Cuban-style. There is rum at every turn on this night; it's not easy being Santa after this party!

MENU

PANCETTA-WRAPPED DATES

BACALAO

SHRIMP TAMALES

MASHED MALANGA

RUM-SPIKED BLACK BEAN SOUP AND WHITE RICE

HERB-STUFFED WHOLE FISH WITH MOJITO GLAZE

RUM RAISIN PUDDING

CHRISTMAS COOKIES

COCONOG BATIDAS

WINE

PORTUGUESE VINTAGE BRUTO

(JP VINHOS LORIDOS)

SERVES 10

Opposite: Herb-Stuffed Whole Fish with Mojito Glaze.

Another example of the exotic influence of Arabia on Spain. A perfect starter for a Christian holiday.

Pancetta-Wrapped Dates

¾ pound pancetta, thinly sliced

30 pitted dates (2 small packages)

30 blanched whole almonds

Preheat oven to 350 degrees.

Using a sharp knife, cut the pancetta slices in half. Stuff each date with an almond and wrap each date in a half slice of pancetta and place on a baking sheet. Bake the dates for 5–8 minutes until the pancetta is just cooked and browned.

Serve the dates warm or at room temperature.

Bacalao

⅓ pound salt cod

1 cup whole milk

1 large Idaho potato

⅔ cup olive oil

5 cloves garlic

Salt and pepper to taste

6–8 slices white bread, crusts removed, toasted

Place the cod in a medium bowl and add milk to cover. Wrap the bowl tightly and allow the cod to soak for at least 24 hours. Strain the cod and rinse under cold water, then soak again in cold water for an additional hour.

In a medium saucepan, place the potato and codfish, cover with cold water, and bring to a boil over medium-high heat until the potato is soft. Pour off the water, place potato in a medium bowl with ⅓ cup olive oil, and mash with a potato masher. In a food processor fitted with the metal blade, puree the codfish with remaining olive oil.

Using the flat of a knife blade or a mortar and pestle, mash the garlic into a paste. Add the codfish puree and garlic to mashed potatoes and blend well. Mix in salt and pepper. Taste to adjust seasoning, adding more olive oil, salt, and pepper if necessary.

To serve, cut the toast slices into 4 triangles per slice. Spread the warm bacalao on the toast points and arrange on a platter.

Cod is found on virtually every Basque menu in Spain. Fortunately, the Basques know myriad ways to prepare it. Here is an especially tasty one.

Andres and Alex.

Shrimp Tamales

FILLING

3 tablespoons olive oil

5 cloves garlic, minced

1 medium onion, chopped

1 roasted green pepper, diced

1 pound roasted tomatillos, diced

1 pound small shrimp, deveined and tails removed, cooked and peeled

$\frac{1}{2}$ cup chopped cilantro

Juice of 1 lime

Salt and pepper to taste

DOUGH

4 cups masa harina

2 teaspoon baking powder

2 teaspoon salt

14 tablespoons shortening or lard, chilled and cut into small pieces

$2\frac{1}{4}$ cups warm chicken stock

1 package of 24 frozen banana leaves

Kitchen string

Prepare filling: Heat oil in heavy skillet and cook garlic and onion until soft, about 3 minutes. Add roasted green pepper, roasted tomatillos, and shrimp. Simmer to meld flavors; about 3 minutes. Drain, transfer to bowl, and cool. Add cilantro, lime juice, salt, and pepper. Cover with plastic wrap and set aside.

To make the dough, combine the masa, baking powder, and salt in a large mixing bowl. Add the shortening or lard to the dry mix and toss to coat the pieces. Using your fingers, rub the shortening or lard into the dry mix until it forms a rough cornmeal texture. Add the warm chicken stock, mixing to form dough. It may be necessary to add water 1 tablespoon at a time until the dough holds together but is not sticky. Divide the dough evenly into 24 pieces.

To make the tamales, cut banana leaves into 8-inch squares. Place the tamale dough in the center of the leaf. Place your filling in the

Isabel with presents.

center of the dough. Fold the bottom of the tamale a quarter of the way up toward the top, and then fold one side into the center to cover the filling and fold second side overlapping the first side. Tie the tamale closed with kitchen string.

In a saucepan, bring water to a boil over medium-high heat. Place the tamales in a steamer basket, cover, and steam for 40–45 minutes.

NOTE: In Cuba tamales are wrapped in banana leaves, but if you can't find banana leaves at your Latino grocer or online, you can use cornhusks, as shown in the Pork Tamales recipe on pages 16–17.

MAKES 24 TAMALES

Mashed Malanga

3   pounds frozen malanga
½   cup (1 stick) unsalted butter, cut into pieces
2   teaspoons dried oregano
Salt and pepper to taste

Place the frozen malanga in a steamer basket, cover, and bring water to a boil over medium-high heat. Steam the malanga until soft, about 30 minutes. In a large bowl, place the malanga, butter, oregano, salt, and pepper and mash with a potato masher until ingredients are combined. Serve hot.

NOTE: Malanga can be hard to work with; the frozen product saves time.

Mateo unwrapping.

A Caribbean classic, this soup is a tradition at Christmas, but we have it as often as possible throughout the year. The variations in this soup can cause an argument not unlike those in our childhood. This version should keep everyone happy.

Rum-Spiked Black Bean Soup and White Rice

2   pounds black beans

12   cups water

4   cups chicken stock

1   bay leaf

4   cloves garlic, minced

2   roasted green bell peppers, chopped

1   onion, finely chopped

1   carrot, peeled and finely chopped

1   celery stalk, finely chopped

¼   cup plus 2 tablespoons olive oil

2   tablespoons red wine vinegar

1   teaspoon sugar

1   teaspoon dried oregano

½   teaspoon cumin

Salt and pepper to taste

Light rum (Bacardi)

Red wine vinegar

Cooked white rice

Carefully pick through the beans and remove any foreign objects. Soak overnight covered with water. Place beans into a colander, rinse under cold water, then transfer to a large stockpot. Add 4 cups water, chicken stock, and bay leaf to the beans. Bring the beans to a boil over high heat, then reduce to medium-high and continue to boil for 45 minutes. Add the remaining water as needed; beans should be covered in liquid at all times during this process.

In a large skillet, sauté the garlic, roasted pepper, onion, carrot, and celery in 2 tablespoons olive oil over medium-high heat until soft. Stir this mixture into the bean soup and allow the beans to continue to cook for an additional 30 minutes.

Check to see if the beans are tender. If they are not, continue simmering, adding water if necessary. Remove the bay leaf.

To finish the soup stir in the ¼ cup olive oil, vinegar, sugar, oregano, cumin, salt, and pepper.

Serve the soup hot with a splash of rum, red wine vinegar, and a little white rice.

Our friend Mario Batali tells us of an Italian tradition of a Christmas Eve with seven seafood dishes representing the seven sacraments. It appears this menu works in Italy or Spain.

Annick shaking a present.

Herb-Stuffed Whole Fish with Mojito Glaze

5   2-pound red snappers, whole

1½ cup mint leaves

1½ cup light rum

1   cup sugar

Juice of 6 limes

4   lemons, thinly sliced

4   limes, thinly sliced

Nonstick cooking spray

1   bunch flat-leaf parsley

1   bunch cilantro

1   bunch oregano

Salt and pepper to taste

Preheat oven to 375 degrees.

Have the fishmonger scale, gut, and clean your fish for you, leaving the head and tail intact.

In a food processor fitted with the metal blade or a blender, mix the mint, rum, sugar, and lime juice. Process until smooth and set the mojito sauce aside.

Grease with nonstick cooking spray 2 roasting pans or casserole dishes large enough to accommodate all the fish. Arrange enough lemon and lime slices to cover the bottom of the pans, reserving 10 slices each of lemon and lime to stuff the fish.

Stuff each fish with alternating lemon and lime slices, topping them with several sprigs of each of the parsley, cilantro, and oregano. Lay the fish evenly spaced on the lemon and lime slices in the roasting pan.

Stir the mojito sauce and pour just enough to glaze each fish. Reserve remaining sauce to glaze again. Roast the fish for 40–60 minutes until the flesh is opaque and flaky. Glaze the fish again after 20–25 minutes.

To serve, work a spatula under fish and arrange on a platter. Pour drippings over fish. Garnish with lemon and lime slices and sprigs of fresh herbs.

Rum Raisin Pudding

³⁄₄ cup raisins

1 cup dark rum

2 cups milk

2 eggs

1¹⁄₂ teaspoon vanilla

¹⁄₂ cup sugar

¹⁄₂ teaspoon cinnamon

¹⁄₂ teaspoon salt

2 cups cooked white rice

2 cups whipped cream

Soak the raisins in ¹⁄₂ cup rum for at least 3 hours or overnight, and drain.

Preheat oven to 350 degrees. Butter an ovenproof bowl.

Heat the milk with ¹⁄₂ cup rum until hot but not boiling. Whisk together the eggs, vanilla, sugar, cinnamon, and salt. While whisking, slowly add ¹⁄₂ cup hot milk and rum to temper the egg mixture, then add the remaining hot milk.

Add the soaked raisins and cooked rice and pour rice pudding into a buttered baking dish. Bake for 30–40 minutes until set. Remove from oven and allow to cool completely.

When rice pudding is cool, fold in the 2 cups of whipped cream. Rice pudding can be made up to 3 days in advance and kept refrigerated in an airtight container.

Javier and Christian.

We are Cuban but we have embraced being American, and what is Christmas without sugar cookies?

Coconog Batida

Part piña colada, part eggnog—a tropical holiday cocktail.

2   ounces white rum

1   ounce dark rum

2   ounces Coco Lopez

1   ounce cream

1   ounce guava nectar

$\frac{1}{2}$ ounce lime juice

Crushed ice

Fresh mint sprigs for garnish

Combine all ingredients in blender and blend. Pour into highball glass and garnish with sprig of mint.

Christmas Cookies

3   cups all-purpose flour

$\frac{3}{4}$ teaspoon baking powder

$\frac{1}{2}$ teaspoon baking soda

$\frac{1}{2}$ teaspoon salt

1   cup (2 sticks) unsalted butter

$1\frac{1}{2}$ cup granulated sugar

2   eggs

2   teaspoons vanilla

ROYAL ICING

1   egg white

1   tablespoon lemon juice

$1\frac{1}{2}$ cup confectioners' sugar

Colored sprinkles

Preheat oven to 350 degrees.

In a medium bowl sift together the flour, baking powder, baking soda, and salt and set aside.

In the bowl of an electric mixer, beat the butter and sugar on high until light and fluffy. Add the eggs one at a time until completely incorporated, then add vanilla.

Turn mixer to low speed and gradually add the flour mixture until just combined. Divide the dough into 3 equal parts, form into disks, and wrap in plastic. Refrigerate for at least one hour.

Roll the dough out on a floured surface to a $\frac{1}{8}$-inch thickness. Use Christmas cookie cutters to cut out shapes and bake on a lightly greased baking sheet for 5–7 minutes until just baked, not browned.

To make the icing, whip the egg white and lemon juice in a medium bowl with an electric mixer or whisk until frothy. Gradually add the confectioners' sugar and beat until glossy. Icing can be made a week in advance and kept refrigerated in an airtight container.

Use a butter knife or small offset spatula to ice the cookies. Add sprinkles. Icing can be piped through a small round tip to outline cookies.

MAKES 3–4 DOZEN COOKIES

Christmas Family Brunch

I married a Texan and my Christmas mornings have been different ever since. The migas are all Amy and an easy breakfast pleaser, the tequila-cured salmon comes from one of our restaurants, and the arepas are as rustic as it gets, unless you include tripe, and we don't. Like everything else in Texas, the Christmas morning meal is big. What Amy doesn't know is that Texas Masons bankrolled the Cuban war against Spain—that's the one with Teddy Roosevelt and the Rough Riders. The triangle in our flag is the Masons' compass, and the lone star, well, you probably guessed by now.

MENU

MIGAS

AREPAS

TEQUILA-CURED SALMON QUESADILLAS

TROPICAL FRUIT SALAD WITH PLAIN YOGURT

BANANA SMOOTHIES

MEXICAN HOT CHOCOLATE

MEXI-CANE COFFEE WITH MINT WHIPPED CREAM

SERVES 8

Above: Isabel lends a helping hand.

Opposite: Fernando gets a lesson from Mateo.

Migas are like a child's version of a recipe. Put all this stuff that sounds great together, smash it up, and mix it all in a bowl. Not unlike our children's finger paintings, the results are beautiful.

Migas

12 eggs

$\frac{1}{3}$ cup milk

2 roasted red bell peppers

2 roasted green bell peppers

$\frac{1}{2}$ cup grated Monterey Jack cheese

Salt and pepper to taste

2 tablespoons olive oil

2 cups crumbled tortilla chips

Salsa

In a large mixing bowl, whisk together the eggs and milk. Stir in the red and green peppers, cheese, salt, and pepper.

Heat a large skillet with 2 tablespoons olive oil over medium-high heat. Stir the tortilla chips into the egg mixture and pour into the hot pan. Using a spatula, scramble the eggs, cooking for about 8 minutes until cooked to desired consistency.

Serve with a heaping spoonful of your favorite salsa.

Arepas

6   tablespoons unsalted butter, melted

6   eggs

1$\frac{1}{2}$ cup milk

1$\frac{1}{2}$ cup fine cornmeal

$\frac{1}{2}$ cup all-purpose flour

$\frac{1}{3}$ cup sugar

1   teaspoon salt

Canola oil for frying

Whipped unsalted butter

Maple syrup

Melt the butter in a small saucepan over medium-high heat and allow to cool. In a medium mixing bowl, whisk together the eggs and milk.

In a large bowl, mix the cornmeal, flour, sugar, and salt, stirring with a fork to blend. Make a well in the center of the cornmeal mixture and add the egg mixture and butter. Quickly stir ingredients together until combined well. Allow the batter to rest for 15 minutes.

In a large heavy skillet, heat 1–2 tablespoons of canola oil over medium-high heat. When the oil is hot but not smoking, spoon batter into skillet to form 3-inch pancakes. Allow the pancakes to cook until browned on bottom, about 1–2 minutes, and using a spatula, flip the pancake over and cook until browned.

Serve the arepas with whipped butter and warm maple syrup.

MAKES ABOUT 24 THREE-INCH PANCAKES OR

12 LARGE PANCAKES

Mateo hopes for the best.

Anyone who lives in New York for a period of time eventually learns to love cured fish. This version has a Mexican twist.

Tequila-Cured Salmon Quesadillas

1-pound salmon fillet

$\frac{1}{2}$ cup sugar

$\frac{1}{2}$ cup kosher salt

$\frac{1}{4}$ cup cracked black pepper

$\frac{1}{3}$ cup añejo tequila

1 bunch fresh oregano, plus $\frac{1}{4}$ cup leaves, chopped

16 small flour tortillas

$1\frac{1}{2}$ cup sour cream

On a cutting board, cut the salmon fillet in half widthwise. In a small bowl combine the sugar, salt, and pepper, stirring with a fork.

On a clean work surface, lay out a piece of plastic wrap large enough to completely enclose the salmon. Place the two salmon pieces skin side down on the plastic. Evenly sprinkle both pieces of salmon with the sugar mixture. Evenly distribute the tequila over the salmon. Use your fingers to rub the tequila paste into the salmon gently, evenly coating it.

Lay the bunch of oregano on one piece of the salmon and place the second piece of salmon on top, flesh side to flesh side. Press down gently on the salmon and wrap tightly in several pieces of plastic wrap.

Place the salmon package in a glass or plastic container and set a large canned product on top of the salmon to press it. Refrigerate for 24 hours to cure, turning once halfway through.

Remove the salmon from the wrapping. Separate the two pieces and discard the oregano. Lightly rinse the salmon under cold water. Pat salmon dry with a paper towel. Using a sharp knife, thinly slice the salmon on a diagonal off the skin.

To make the quesadillas, heat a large skillet over medium-high heat. Arrange 3–4 pieces of salmon on a tortilla, cover with 3 tablespoons of sour cream, and sprinkle with a pinch of chopped oregano. Top with a second tortilla and place in the pan. Heat the quesadilla until the tortilla is lightly browned. Using a spatula, flip the quesadilla over and brown the other side.

To serve the quesadillas, cut them into quarters and serve warm.

Tropical Fruit Salad
with Plain Yogurt

1   fresh pineapple, peeled, cored, and cubed

1   papaya, peeled and cubed

1   mango, peeled and cubed

1   cup red grapes, sliced in half lengthwise

1   cup cubed honeydew melon

¼   cup lime juice

2   tablespoons dark rum

2   tablespoons chopped fresh mint, plus 2 sprigs for garnish

1   tablespoon confectioners' sugar

2–3 cups plain yogurt

In a large nonreactive bowl, combine the pineapple, papaya, mango, grapes, and honeydew melon, tossing gently. Add the lime juice and rum, then sprinkle the chopped mint and sugar over the fruit. Toss the fruit to combine. Serve chilled, garnished with fresh mint leaves. Serve the yogurt on the side in a separate bowl.

NOTE: Can be made 1–2 hours ahead of time.

Isabel and Mateo on Christmas morning.

Banana Smoothies

8 ripe bananas

2$\frac{1}{2}$ cups vanilla or banana yogurt

$\frac{1}{2}$ cup milk

2 cups ice cubes

1 teaspoon nutmeg (optional)

Make the smoothies in two batches. In the jar of a blender, place 4 bananas, 1$\frac{1}{4}$ cup yogurt, $\frac{1}{4}$ cup milk, 1 cup ice cubes, and $\frac{1}{2}$ teaspoon nutmeg. Blend on high until smooth. You can use more or less milk to reach the consistency you prefer.

MAKES EIGHT 6-OUNCE GLASSES

Mexican Hot Chocolate

4 cups milk

2 Ibarra sweet chocolate disks, chopped

Pinch cinnamon

Whipped cream (optional)

In a heavy saucepan, heat the milk over medium heat until hot but not boiling. Add the chocolate and stir until dissolved. Add a pinch of cinnamon and stir.

Serve hot with whipped cream.

NOTE: We gave a brand name for this recipe because Ibarra is the best. Try to find its distinctive yellow and maroon box, or order online.

SERVES 4

Mexi-Cane Coffee with Mint Whipped Cream

1 ounce Kahlúa

1 ounce dark rum

4 ounces coffee

Mint whipped cream

Combine spirits in coffee cup, fill with coffee, and top with mint whipped cream.

MINT WHIPPED CREAM

$\frac{1}{2}$ pint whipping cream

2 drops vanilla

5 mint leaves, shredded

Whip cream with vanilla into peaks. Stir mint in.

Mateo heading out.

Spanish Winter Family Dinner

Simple and easy with lots of flavor is the order of the day for weeknights. The garlicky potatoes could be our favorite dish. Our sister learned to make these fries when she was in college at La Universidad de Navarre in Pamplona, Spain. Maite makes them whenever we visit her in Los Angeles.

Maite was not the only one from our family who spent a lot of time in Spain. The whole family went to Barcelona for the Olympic Games as Alvaro was publisher of *Sports Illustrated* at the time.

Above: During rare visits to Long Island in the winter, we have the beach to ourselves.

Opposite: Maite's Basque Flag Pepper-and-Garlic Fries and Chorizo-Fig-and-Spanish-Olive-Stuffed Pork Loin.

MENU

CATALAN SPINACH

MAITE'S BASQUE FLAG PEPPER-AND-GARLIC FRIES

CHORIZO-FIG-AND-SPANISH-OLIVE-STUFFED PORK LOIN

BANANA SPLITS WITH TRES LECHES ICE CREAM AND RUM CARAMEL SAUCE

SARALEGUI SANGRIA

WINE
RED WINE SANGRIA
(BODEGAS DOMINIO DE EGUREN PROTOCOLO TINTO)

SERVES 4 TO 6

Catalan Spinach

2 tablespoons olive oil

5 cloves garlic, sliced

2 large bunches of spinach, washed, dried, and
chopped or 2 six-ounce bags of baby spinach

¼ cup toasted pine nuts

¼ cup currants

In a large sauté pan, heat the olive oil over medium-high heat and sauté the garlic for 30 seconds. Add half the spinach and toss with tongs until wilted. Add the pine nuts and currants and the remaining spinach and toss until just cooked. Serve immediately.

Mateo and Amy enjoy a cool day on the beach.

Maite's Basque Flag Pepper-and-Garlic Fries

6   cups vegetable oil

6   Idaho potatoes, washed but not peeled

3   green bell peppers, cored and seeded

4   cloves garlic, thinly sliced

Salt and pepper to taste

At our restaurants, family favorites always made it onto the menus, and this recipe was no exception. I guarantee, if you like garlic, you too will love this dish.

Line a baking sheet with several layers of paper towels. Using a candy thermometer, heat the oil in a tall, large, heavy stockpot to 380 degrees. If you don't have a thermometer, heat the oil until hot; to check if it's ready for frying, add one piece of potato—it should sizzle like crazy and float.

While the oil is heating, slice the potatoes into thick steak-cut potato sticks. Slice the bell peppers into thick slices equal to the potato sticks. In a large bowl, combine the potato sticks and pepper slices.

Once the oil is hot, in 3–4 batches, add the potato sticks and pepper slices together, wait 30 seconds, add sliced garlic, and fry until golden brown. Remove the fries, pepper, and garlic with tongs and allow them to drain on the paper-towel-lined baking sheet, immediately sprinkling with salt and pepper. Allow the oil to return to 350 degrees before adding each additional batch. Keep the fried potatoes warm in a 375–degree oven while frying the remaining batches.

Serve immediately.

Chorizo-Fig-and-Spanish-Olive-Stuffed Pork Loin

2   small (approximately 3$\frac{1}{2}$ ounces) chorizo sausages, chopped

$\frac{1}{2}$ cup pitted green Spanish olives

$\frac{1}{2}$ teaspoon salt

$\frac{1}{2}$ teaspoon cracked black pepper

$\frac{1}{2}$ teaspoon dried oregano

4   small mission figs, quartered

2   1$\frac{1}{2}$-pound pork tenderloins

2   tablespoons olive oil

Kitchen string

Preheat oven to 350 degrees.

In a food processor fitted with the metal blade, combine chorizo, olives, salt, pepper, and oregano, pulsing until it resembles a rough mash. Add the figs and pulse 3–5 times to just incorporate the figs but not mash them.

Using a sharp knife, slice the pork tenderloins down the center lengthwise, about three quarters of the way through. Stuff the pork tenderloins with the fig filling. Tie the pork tenderloins closed with kitchen string in 1-inch intervals.

In a large, heavy skillet, brown pork tenderloins in the olive oil over high heat. Transfer the pork loin to a roasting pan and roast in the oven for 20–30 minutes until an instant-read thermometer reads 165 degrees when inserted into the center of the meat.

Allow the pork loin to rest for 10 minutes, loosely covered with aluminum foil, before slicing. Cut kitchen string from pork before serving.

NOTE: Whenever there are pork leftovers, never miss the opportunity to make a Cuban Ruban (page 130).

Banana Splits with Tres Leches Ice Cream and Rum Caramel Sauce

$1\frac{1}{3}$ cup dark brown sugar

$\frac{1}{3}$ cup ($\frac{3}{4}$ stick) unsalted butter

$\frac{1}{2}$ cup heavy cream

1 teaspoon vanilla

2 tablespoons dark rum

6 ripe bananas

1 pint Häagen Dazs Dulce de Leche ice cream

In a heavy medium saucepan, melt the brown sugar and butter together over medium heat. When sugar is completely dissolved, stir in the heavy cream and vanilla until well blended. Remove from heat and stir in the rum.

To prepare the bananas, peel and slice in half lengthwise.

To assemble the banana splits, place 1 banana in each of 6 bowls. Using an ice cream scoop, put 2 scoops of ice cream in between the banana slices. Generously pour the caramel sauce over the banana splits and serve immediately.

Caramel sauce can be served warm or chilled and can be made 3 days in advance and kept refrigerated in an airtight container.

Saralegui Sangria

3 bottles of red wine (Gamay)

1 quart orange juice

1 pint lemon juice

$1\frac{1}{2}$ cup gold rum (Mt. Gay)

Club soda

4 limes, quartered

2 apples, cored and sliced

2 oranges, sliced in circles

Combine wine, orange juice, lemon juice, and rum in a pitcher and chill. Serve in a wineglass, top with splash of club soda, and garnish with fruit.

RESOURCES

Whether you're in the middle of nowhere or just lazy, this guide
will help you find what you need through catalogs or online.

Amazonas Imports, Inc.
10817 Sherman Way
Sun Valley, CA 91352
818-982-1377
www.peimco.com

Dean & Deluca
Mail Order Department
560 Broadway
New York, NY 10012
212-431-1691
877-826-9246 toll-free
www.dean-deluca.com

Cubanfoodmarket.com
3100 SW 8 Street
Miami, FL 33135
877-999-9945 toll-free
www.cubanfoodmarket.com

Enchanted Seeds
P.O. Box 6087
Las Cruces, NM 88006
505-523-6058
www.enchantedseeds.com

EthnicGrocer
695 Lunt Avenue
Elk Grove, IL 60007
847-640-9570
866-438-4642 toll-free
www.ethnicgrocer.com

Frieda's, Inc.
4465 Corporate Center Drive
Los Alamitos, CA 90720
800-241-1771 toll-free
www.friedas.com

**G. B. Ratto's International
Market & Deli**
821 Washington Street
Oakland, CA 94607
510-832-6503

Going Bananas
24401 SW 197 Avenue
Homestead, FL 33031
305-247-0397
www.going-bananas.com

Gypsy Kitchen (previously
Le Saucier in Faneuil Hall)
1214 Hancock Street
Quincy, MA 02169
617-847-1846
www.drhot.net

La Espanola Meats, Inc.
25020 Doble Avenue
Harbor City, CA 90710
310-539-0455
www.donajuana.com

La Guadalupana
4637 S. Archer Avenue
Chicago, IL 60632
773-843-1722

**Melissa's World Variety
Produce, Inc.**
P.O. Box 21127
Los Angeles, CA 90021
800-588-0151 toll-free
www.melissas.com

Michael Skurnik Wines
575 Underhill Boulevard,
Suite 216
Syosset, NY 11791
516-677-9300
www.skurnikwines.com

Pepper Gal
P.O. Box 23006
Ft. Lauderdale, FL 33307
954-537-5540

Raymond-Hadley Peruvian Foods
89 Tompkins Street
Spencer, NY 14883
800-252-5220 toll-free
607-589-4415
www.raymondhadley.com

INDEX

Page numbers in *italics* indicate illustrations.